More Praise for *From PMO to VMO*

"*From PMO to VMO* provides a clear vision of how to make value tangible inside your organization—and more importantly, how to do so with the teams and capabilities that already exist. By the end of this book, you will understand what is valuable, how to measure value, and how to optimize for the flow of value—from idea to your customer."

—**Evan Leybourn, cofounder and CEO, Business Agility Institute**

"This book fills the knowledge gap that exists within so many companies of how to effectively manage a lean-agile delivery system at scale. It is a great achievement of balancing the need for portfolio management and discipline with nimble and fast-moving teams."

—**Thomas Paider, Fortune 100 technology executive and coauthor of *The Lean IT Field Guide***

"*From PMO to VMO* lays out a road map to expand your agile transformation well beyond the walls of IT. The book provides compelling evidence and concrete actions senior IT leaders should follow to improve the speed, quality, and efficiency of overall delivery."

—**Kevin G. Fisher, former Associate Vice President, Lean IT, Nationwide Insurance**

"A vision and a road map for transforming the traditional PMO into a refreshing model of Agile Value Management Office (Agile VMO) that focuses on measuring, prioritizing, and delivering customer value. If you are a project manager or work with a PMO, this is a must-read to help you navigate the future of organizational agility."

—**Dr. Rashina Hoda, "Voice of Agile Research," Associate Professor, Monash University**

"It is a challenge to keep up with all the significant developments from lean, agile, and design thinking and then see where they fit in a busy PMO. *From PMO to VMO* lays out all the major building blocks and explains how they fit together to create a modern, functioning VMO that adds value and supports both teams and the business."

—**Mike Griffiths, CEO, Leading Answers Inc., and author of *Beyond Agile***

"Once again, Sanjiv Augustine is at the vanguard of organizational thinking—always focusing on the why, not just the *what* and *how*. This book is a practical road map for adopting an agile, value-driven approach to managing the output of your organization."

—**Max Keeler, Senior Techie at Large, The Motley Fool**

T0333953

"I've been leading agile teams for over fifteen years. Each leg in my journey to learn and impart agility has felt like steps toward something better, but steps to what exactly? This excellent book finally explains, with much clarity, the point of it all."

—Don Sargent, CTO, *Chronicle of Higher Education*

"This comprehensive guide combines the distinctions of lean-agile processes and enterprise management science to create a value-driven engine for enterprise agility. As a bonus, it is easily applicable to any agile/scaling framework. Managers and leadership will learn how to shift focus from managing to maximizing value and how to utilize the existing structure for building the desired outcome. Highly recommended."

—Deepti Jain, founder of AgileVirgin and India Agile Community Development Chief, Agile Alliance

FROM PMO
TO VMO

FROM PMO TO VMO

Managing for Value Delivery

Sanjiv Augustine

Roland Cuellar

Audrey Scheere

BK®

Berrett–Koehler Publishers, Inc.

Berrett-Koehler Publishers, Inc.
1333 Broadway, Suite 1000
Oakland, CA 94612-1921
Tel: (510) 817-2277
Fax: (510) 817-2278
www.bkconnection.com

ORDERING INFORMATION

Quantity sales. Special discounts are available on quantity purchases by corporations, associations, and others. For details, contact the "Special Sales Department" at the Berrett-Koehler address above.

Individual sales. Berrett-Koehler publications are available through most bookstores. They can also be ordered directly from Berrett-Koehler: Tel: (800) 929-2929; Fax: (802) 864-7626; www.bkconnection.com.

Orders for college textbook / course adoption use. Please contact Berrett-Koehler: Tel: (800) 929-2929; Fax: (802) 864-7626.

Distributed to the U.S. trade and internationally by Penguin Random House Publisher Services.

Berrett-Koehler and the BK logo are registered trademarks of Berrett-Koehler Publishers, Inc.

Printed in the United States of America

Berrett-Koehler books are printed on long-lasting acid-free paper. When it is available, we choose paper that has been manufactured by environmentally responsible processes. These may include using trees grown in sustainable forests, incorporating recycled paper, minimizing chlorine in bleaching, or recycling the energy produced at the paper mill.

CIP data for this book is available at the Library of Congress.
ISBN: 978-1-5230-9136-2

First Edition

27 26 25 24 23 22 21   10 9 8 7 6 5 4 3 2 1

Book producer: Westchester Publishing Services
Cover designer: Kim Scott

Our friend and colleague Roland Cuellar
passed away on April 29, 2021.

Roland, we dedicate this book to you with the deepest of
sorrow, the fondest of memories, and the highest of respect.
We were singularly blessed to know you and to share this earthly
sojourn with you. In the infinite arc of the universe, we will
surely journey together again.

Sanjiv:
To Sujatha, Sameer, Sandhya, and our families

Roland:
To Alison and Tony, I am forever grateful

Audrey:
To D, B, and G

Contents

Tables

Figures

Foreword

Scott Ambler
Vice President, Chief Scientist of Disciplined
Agile at Project Management Institute

Mark Lines
Vice President, Disciplined Agile at Project
Management Institute

SCOTT: We need to get going on writing the foreword for *From PMO to VMO*.

MARK: Agreed. How should we go about it?

SCOTT: I'm thinking that we write it as a chat stream. Given that everyone is working remotely these days, they'll be able to relate to it better than if we wrote straightforward prose.

MARK: Seems gimmicky.

SCOTT: Sure, but all we need to do is spin a story about turbulent business conditions, yadda yadda yadda, new ways of working, blah blah blah, and people will go for it.

MARK: Yeah. . . . Not so sure this'll fly, but let's try it. Where should we start?

SCOTT: First thing we should address is why someone should read this book. What struck you as the key learnings?

MARK: The critical point is that project management offices need to evolve, and they need to do it now. The authors are right in their observation that PMOs are struggling and often under attack in many organizations. To be fair, if PMOs aren't adding value, if they are not helping their organization to improve, then they should be under attack. We've both seen this in practice, particularly in the IT space where PMOs tend to be an obstacle to agile rather than a conduit for it. On the other hand, the most effective agile transformations that we have seen usually involved the PMO stepping up and being actively involved with the transformation and often driving it.

SCOTT: That's it exactly. In some ways it's like Schrödinger's PMO, where you don't know if the PMO is an ally or an enemy until you open the box and see what's inside. This book presents a sharp vision for how PMOs can become a valuable and, better yet, a strategic group within their enterprise. PMOs do this by evolving into value management offices (VMOs), reflecting that it's not just about successfully delivering projects anymore—and arguably it never was. In agile enterprises, or Disciplined Agile enterprises, it's about identifying and nurturing endeavors that add value to the organization and for customers. Someone still needs to guide and oversee these endeavors, and that's a key role of a VMO. This mindset reflects the latest thinking of the Project Management Institute and other industry leaders.

MARK: I agree, I think this book changes the way that people will think about PMOs.

SCOTT: As you said, this book really confirms what we have been seeing for the past few years, and it has certainly accelerated recently with COVID-19 forcing organizations to get serious about their way of working (WoW). What I like about it most is that it provides a clear strategy for existing PMOs to get it together, to align themselves with the rest of the organization. The VMO strategy described in this book ties together several advanced topics such as the need for ensuring effective governance, guiding a range of endeavors executed by teams working via unique fit-for-purpose WoWs, and of course, working smarter.

MARK: You and I have pointed out that functional support areas such as PMOs generally do not choose to be impediments to solution delivery teams' agility. The reality is that no one has taken the time to teach them new, more modern ways of working. In our experience it is relatively straightforward to apply the techniques described in this book for removing process waste and streamlining delivery of value to customers without increasing risk. Applying these lean ways of working invariably creates joy for PMOs because the new methods are frankly more fun than the old. A typical example we have seen in the past is moving from exhaustive business cases, which are often elaborate works of fiction with questionable costs and benefits, to a one-page lean business case canvas. Much less work and usually as, or more, accurate.

SCOTT: The wonderful thing about this book is how well it ties back to what we are doing in PMI's **Disciplined Agile**™ (DA) tool kit.

MARK: Exactly. The **DA**™ toolkit explicitly describes how organizations offer value streams to their customers, going into greater detail and supplying options that your VMO can use. Just as this book argues that VMOs need to govern agile teams in an agile manner and traditional teams in a traditional manner, so does Disciplined Agile. We've all had similar experiences and are coming from the same point of view—we want to share what works in practice, not what we hope will work in theory. And of course, agile portfolio management that takes more of a continuous approach to strategy and planning, rather than the annual approaches of the past, is a critical component for VMO success.

SCOTT: You took the words right out of my mouth. Something I cannot stress enough is the need to recognize that teams are unique and will need to work in a fit-for-purpose manner that is unique to them. A 5-person project team will work differently than a 90-person program. A short-term project team will work differently than a long-standing project team. A team focused on integrating a new software package into infrastructure will work differently than a team focused on directly interacting with customers. These teams need guidance and nurturing from leadership that gets it. This book is a blueprint for PMOs to become organizational leaders once again.

MARK: Writing the foreword as if it were a chat worked out well.

SCOTT: It was gimmicky, though.

MARK: Totally. We should end by telling people to read this book and then act on its advice.

SCOTT: Good point. You should read this book and then act on this advice.

Scott Ambler and Mark Lines are the cocreators of the Disciplined Agile tool kit of the Project Management Institute and coauthors of several books, including *Choose Your WoW! A Disciplined Agile Delivery Handbook for Optimizing Your Way of Working* and *An Executive's Guide to Disciplined Agile: Winning the Race to Business Agility.*

As the agile movement hits the 20-year mark, the role of middle management remains undefined and the traditional project manager is denounced as antiagile in many quarters. Project managers are often made out to be villains, draconian keepers of the "plan" and blockers of organizational agility.

In the midst of a lot of snake oil being peddled, the project management field and project managers in particular are being needlessly ostracized. Project managers are not the destroyers of all things agile. In fact, the agile community has often missed opportunities to make use of the unique skill sets of project managers and the strengths of the players in the project management office (PMO).

We are executive consultants who have been in the heart of agile for two decades. We have heard from senior leaders across industries that "project managers are running for their lives," and have seen hundreds of project manager positions being thoughtlessly eliminated. We believe that this is a big mistake and will have many negative ramifications down the line.

We have a history of holding project manager responsibilities and have been a part of the Project Management Institute–Agile Certified Practitioner movement since its inception. We understand the plight of the project manager in agile, and with our unique point of view, we feel the burden and a pull to represent this part of the business community.

We have been helping the PMO evolve since the early 2000s, when two of us wrote "The Lean-Agile PMO,"[1] then suggesting how to combine agile project delivery at the project level with lean thinking at the portfolio level. Building on that through the years, we have seen that whichever methodology is being implemented, success at all levels is inextricably linked back to a clear understanding of customer value and customer-driven outcomes across teams.

In all kinds of organizations, executives have told us over and over that this is where they struggle—this cross-team layer is a clear and unfulfilled need in their organizations. They have agile teams, they have agile initiatives, leadership has bought in, but the barriers are many. They can't tie initiatives back to customer value and outcomes. In short, they can't get value to flow across teams, programs, and portfolios.

Project managers and the PMO have a valuable new role to play in this space through an exciting organizational construct—the Agile Value Management Office (Agile VMO®). Rather than running for their lives, organizations that embrace the skills of their project managers and PMOs have a well-equipped VMO team ready to decide the best ways to connect processes to value and to get value flowing rapidly. This is especially urgent as organizations across the world have embraced virtual work in a big way during the pandemic and are likely to continue large-scale virtual work well into the future.

It's impossible to go anywhere without a vision and a road map. We hope this book helps you envision a reality where project managers and middle management are leveraged for their strengths and for the benefit of all—individuals and organizations alike. We have provided as many real case studies and step-by-step paths as possible for you to visualize and implement this new path: where middle management and the VMO are valued leaders in the age of business agility.

Sanjiv, Roland, and Audrey
Alexandria, Virginia; Arlington, Virginia; and Tucson, Arizona
Spring 2021

1 ■ Introducing the Agile VMO

On March 11, 2020, the World Health Organization declared the rapidly spreading coronavirus outbreak a pandemic. If you, like us, were among the millions around the world watching news reports with growing dread, the WHO's announcement was merely a confirmation that the world we knew was about to be rocked by the biggest "black swan" event in over a century.

Years and perhaps even decades from now, the struggle to minimize the personal, public health, and financial impacts of the pandemic will continue. Each of us will recollect some particular memories of this unprecedented time. In the United States, there will be troubling memories of the federal government's inadequate response and its resulting tragic human and economic impacts. By contrast, the shining examples of state governors in the United States, as well as the governments of Mongolia, Vietnam, Ghana, Trinidad and Tobago, South Korea, and New Zealand, are inspiring case studies in leadership and agility.

Like many governments, most organizations also have historically dealt with layers of red tape, internal politics, and regulations that weigh them down, slowing both innovation and the ability to confront crisis. What we are facing today is the clearest need we have ever seen for organizations in all industries to adapt and pivot quickly. Even as we debate the public examples of pandemic response, examples of business agility are lesser known because they do not make the news headlines.

Out of necessity, businesses small and large along with government agencies have responded with alacrity. Sit-down restaurants have become mini grocery stores, mom-and-pop shops have curbside pickup, and movie theaters are reembracing drive-in shows. Stretching to support these businesses are financial institutions, which processed more loans in the first weeks of April 2020 than they did during all of 2019. In a mind-bending display of mission agility, the U.S. Small Business Administration partnered with these institutions to process *29 years' worth of loans* in April and May 2020.[1] Across the board, enterprises are faced with the slap-in-the-face realization that their business will never be back to the old prepandemic normal. With their revenues dropping by up to 90 percent, the airline and tourism industries will be reeling for decades. We are beginning to settle into the next normal of continued business downturn and public health uncertainty.

Even before this crisis, the average company was facing a challenge unlike any before. As shown in figure 1.1, Innosight predicted that 75 percent of the companies listed on the S&P 500 Index would be replaced by 2027, with the average company tenure trending toward 12 years, down from 60 years in the 1950s.[2]

For decades, technology has broken down barriers between industries and markets, increasing competition and redefining what is possible on a continuous basis. At the same time, lead times to satisfy customers have become much shorter, with constant demands for more value delivered more quickly. This turbulent business environment can be explained by the concept of VUCA (volatility, uncertainty, complexity, and ambiguity), originally coined by the U.S. Army War College to articulate Cold War conditions. In a few

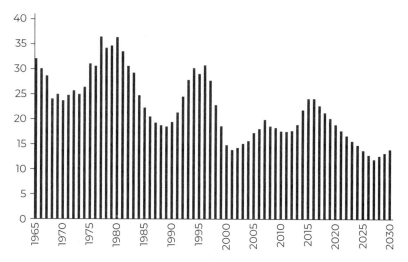

Figure 1.1: *Average company life span on the S&P 500 Index (adapted with permission from Innosight)*

short weeks, the coronavirus pandemic forced all of us violently into a hyper-VUCA world.

The only way for organizations to survive in this next normal is to deliver results more quickly, reducing the time from need to solution to its absolute minimum. Then they need to quickly adapt as necessary to converge on fit-to-purpose solutions to ever-changing customer needs. Digital technologies are rapidly redefining product development and collaboration in this turbulent landscape, and automation and globalization issues are driving business disruption. Overnight, Zoom became our virtual platform of choice and our lifeline for connecting with one another. Now that working from home has become the norm, businesses grapple with employee burnout and productivity concerns as the delineation between work and home life has all but disappeared. To survive in the short term and prosper into the future, businesses are rapidly adapting their strategies, culture, processes, and platforms.

These turbulent business conditions require clear strategy, rapid delivery, an adaptive mindset, and continuous improvement, all steered by strong leadership. Even as vaccines arrive and we begin to overcome the pandemic devastation, we know that turbulence will persist post COVID. Over the past two decades, many chief information officers and other C-suite executives had already built a foundation for business agility by launching initiatives to shorten up-front planning cycles, reduce project size, and increase speed to market by adopting agile methods (see sidebar) in some fashion.

Basics of Agile Methods

Team-Based Agile Methods

Formalized in 2001 via the Agile Manifesto, team-based Agile methods, including Scrum, extreme programming, Crystal, and feature-driven development, provide techniques for delivering customer value while creating agility through rapid iterative and incremental delivery, flexibility, and a focus on customer outcomes. Developed some years later, the Kanban method stressed flow and work-in-progress management to improve speed and throughput. Some of the basic techniques employed by team-based agile methodologies are listed here.

Small releases. Work is divided into small chunks to manage complexity and to get early feedback from customers and end users. Releases are usually delivered in one to three months.

Iterative and incremental development. Plans, requirements, design, product increments, and tests are evolved incrementally through multiple passes, or iterations, rather than through a single waterfall pass with lockdowns of each. Iterations (also called Sprints) are fixed length, usually around two weeks each to maximize feedback, and are fixed scope to retain stability.

Physical or virtual collocation. All team members are collocated physically or using a virtual collaboration tool to facilitate face-to-face communication and rich interactions. Dedicated team rooms are provided for impromptu meetings, design sessions, and other formal and informal group activities.

Product backlog. Desired features are defined at a high level and prioritized by a product owner in a product backlog. The prioritization is done collaboratively with teams. Team members provide level-of-effort estimates, and product owners decide business priority on an ongoing basis in backlog-refinement working sessions. Product owners use the product backlog to create release road maps and release plans.

Sprint/iteration backlog. High-level features from the release plan are elaborated upon and prioritized along with their implementation tasks in a Sprint or iteration backlog. The prioritization is done collaboratively with team members in a Sprint/iteration planning session. Team members provide level-of-effort estimates, and customers decide business priority.

Self-disciplined teams. Team members self-organize by continuously completing tasks collaboratively from the backlogs without top-down management control.

Flow and work-in-progress management. Agile teams visualize their flow of work, limit work in progress, and continuously identify and resolve constraints to improve speed and throughput.

Simple, lean, and adaptable. All aspects of work, including processes, are kept simple, lean (low on wastes), and adaptable to maximize customer value and to accommodate change.

Scaled Agile Methods
Scaled agile methods—including the Scaled Agile Framework (SAFe), Disciplined Agile, Scrum at Scale, Large-Scale

(*continued*)

Scrum (LeSS), and Nexus—extend Scrum, extreme programming, and to a large extent Kanban. They facilitate organizing and coordinating multiple teams into larger cohesive programs for alignment, and they link their work to strategic themes and financial portfolios for oversight, governance, and the delivery of end-to-end business outcomes.

Increasingly, DevOps practices are embedded into both team-based and scaled methods. DevOps is a blend of mindset, culture, practices, and tools that drives the rapid delivery of applications and services. A DevOps platform creates the capability for organizations to deliver, measure and improve customer outcomes.

Now, in our current pandemic era, these leaders are guiding their companies out of the crisis and into the future by building on that agile foundation. They are continuing to grow and evolve their organizations by building on the trust, transparency, and collaboration that agile methods enable. With intentional end-to-end communication, agile methods enable them to understand true customer needs in order to learn and move faster to produce innovative and in-demand products and services. Leaders have also integrated agile methods and expanded them with lean thinking, DevOps, and the cloud to deliver business outcomes. This is the essence of business agility: measuring, learning, and adapting rapidly to deliver desired business outcomes, as illustrated in figure 1.2.

Middle Management Is the Keeper of the Execution Model

By 2020, organizations of all sizes had made visible shifts toward agility. Most organizations that have adopted agile have implemented Scrum, extreme programming, Kanban, and other team-based agile methods. Many have also scaled agile methods up to the program

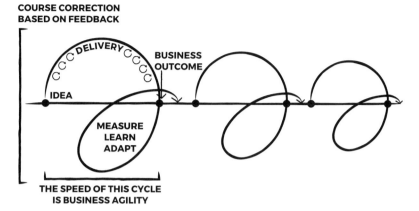

Figure 1.2: *Business agility—measuring, learning, and improving*

and portfolio levels with the Scaled Agile Framework, Disciplined Agile, Large-Scale Scrum, Nexus, or Scrum at Scale.

Scaling these methods from information technology teams to programs and portfolios has not been enough. Even before the pandemic crisis, pioneering companies like Haier Group in China and the Vinci Group in France were forging ahead with postbureaucratic management. They had blown up their bureaucracy and top-down hierarchies, instead employing small, self-managing teams connected via entrepreneurial networks. See chapter 7 for more on Haier's approach. Can we emulate these pioneers in business agility? Perhaps, but the road to success is arduous; it requires clarity of vision, constancy of purpose, and courage and persistence in the execution of a new operating model.

Work management, organizational systems, and policies in most companies are not appropriately structured to allow value to flow across the organization. Instead, in these legacy organizations, every single process, organizational structure, and role is designed to support the current and likely traditional method of delivery. Locked into the past, these rigid, hidebound structures stifle the innovation and agility crucial for an organization to succeed. This is Conway's law[3] writ large—organizations design systems that mirror their own communication structure—and something we must urgently overcome in our current crisis environment.

Sadly, in our decades of experience supporting agile change management, we have seen that individuals in middle management roles tend to offer the stiffest resistance to this critically needed change. These middle managers and junior executives are the gateway between employees in the trenches and top executives in the C-suite who determine strategy. This frozen middle, as it is referred to in management circles, is entrusted with owning the execution model of any strategy or process. They are the ones most invested in the status quo, having worked hard to gain their current position, with years and sometime decades invested in the legacy organizational models. Critically, as organizations transition to a newer end-to-end agile operating model, the roles of middle management need to change to unfreeze the frozen middle. Specifically, these roles will need to be adapted to support agile teams and lead the rapid delivery of value. With such a change, middle management can be freed to champion and lead change, rather than being restricted in organizational structures and roles that impede it. These changes are quite dramatic and must be brought about by executive leaders who understand that they are critical to the survival of their organizations and who have the courage of conviction and the temerity to implement radical change at all levels.

As a cocustodian of the legacy models, project management offices (PMOs) desperately need reinvention as well. Originating in the 1800s as project offices and gaining widespread acceptance and application in the 1900s, contemporary PMOs unfortunately still retain vestiges of legacy industrial-age models, with adherence to bygone practices like implementing rigid, top-down management by objectives or enforcing the iron triangle (cost, time, scope) on projects even as they fail to deliver customer value. As the world has moved on to newer evolutions like quarterly objectives and key results and transitioned from a project to a product model, PMOs remain mired in the past. They have thus become too closely associated with past failures and are not typically identified with newer agile methods or even with postbureaucratic management in general.

PMOs Are under Attack

As organizations become more adaptable and responsive, they are starting to adopt more of a product mindset, which calls into question the need for projects at all. Projects are, after all, an internal construct. Our customers do not care about our projects, our budgets, or even our controls. What they care most about are solutions to their problems through the timely delivery of value, as represented by product features and fixes or service innovations. Because of this fundamental difference in focus, and because PMOs are not associated with newer models of business agility, they are coming under increasing scrutiny and are being pressured to justify their existence in the new age of agile.

Consider the following:

- Project management as a role and as a function is being attacked for being slow, bureaucratic, costly, and at times ineffective. Project management is also unfortunately quite closely linked to waterfall execution models.
- Agile ways of working are quickly leaving the old waterfall execution paradigm behind, making the tools and techniques of most project managers and PMOs more and more irrelevant.
- New roles such as product owners, scrum masters, and release train engineers are starting to chip away at some of the traditional duties of the project manager.
- DevOps and automation tools are starting to provide extreme levels of visibility into progress and quality, lessening the need for traditional forms of reporting.
- The relentless pursuit of cost cutting, profit, and growth makes any function that does not directly add value a potential target for downsizing.

The result of these and other forces is that the traditional PMO and the project managers within it are increasingly under attack, even in the public sector or large and highly regulated private-sector firms. The classical PMO, too closely wedded to management models popular in the 1950s and to waterfall execution in the current age, needs to embrace transformation to stay relevant or to even exist in an agile organization.

Paradoxically, even as middle management is popularly identified with bureaucracy and rigidity, middle managers have been identified as pivotal leaders of successful change management efforts.[4] In the 2020s pandemic era, many organizations worldwide will be struggling to emerge from the crisis in a turbulent sea of rapid and continuous change, even as other, nimbler organizations navigate the crisis successfully. Middle management in general and the PMO in particular have a rare opportunity to lead change from the front and drive value, instead of fading further into obscurity and obsolescence.

Transforming the PMO into an Agile VMO

How can the PMO lead in the modern pandemic age? How can the PMO repurpose itself and redesign its mission and operation to be more value adding, less bureaucratic, more customer focused, and more in line with agile product management and other modern ways of working? We believe that, to accomplish this, the PMO needs to rapidly evolve into the Agile Value Management Office, or Agile VMO®. This transition will represent a huge change for most organizations, and they must provide a formal structure to guide the PMO's evolution into the Agile VMO.

As illustrated in figure 1.3, the VMO's formal structure consists of a small, cross-functional, cross-hierarchy team with key representatives who work collaboratively across the organization.

The VMO has members who function as linking pins across organizational silos and between hierarchical levels. These members will have roles in both the VMO and their organizational units and will ensure tight linkages between the VMO and those organizational units. The key roles in the VMO are director, program manager, and executive champion. The VMO includes executive action team stakeholders, value stream managers, and agile team representatives from across value streams and teams. In chapter 9 we provide a detailed explanation of how to implement this structure in your organization.

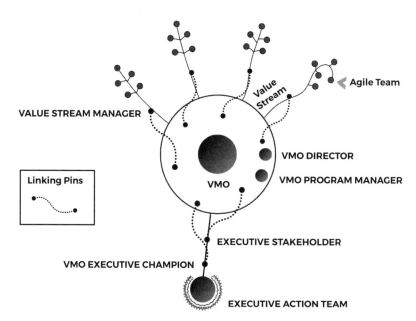

Figure 1.3: *The Agile VMO—an end-to-end, cross-hierarchy team driving business agility*

Achieving true end-to-end business agility requires transitioning to this new Agile VMO structure, as well as the methodical restructuring of processes and structures along the entire value stream, from business strategy to operations and every step along the way.

The VMO has a strategic responsibility to drive organizational change and the day-to-day responsibility to help manage a dynamic, active portfolio of work in partnership with value stream managers. All the VMO's work functions and its members' corresponding responsibilities are listed in table 1.1.

We will cover these in detail in the rest of the book and summarize them in chapter 9. As an applied example, figure 1.4 illustrates how this plays out with Disciplined Agile's program life cycle for a team of teams. As a team of teams, the VMO can help agile teams using Disciplined Agile define their way-of-working processes, help them optimize flow, provide program oversight and governance, and support program coordination.[5]

Table 1.1. *VMO Responsibilities*

Agile VMO Function	Responsibilities
Defining an agile process	• Establish high discipline as the driving goal for all your agile processes • Take a calibrated approach to defining your agile processes • Define metrics that support and drive dynamic transformation • Develop process controls as natural outputs of the process
Organizing around value streams	• Organize as adaptive networks of teams • Define flexible value streams by customer journeys • Establish the VMO as a team of teams • Fund experience-aligned teams by value stream
Adaptive planning	• Conform to value, rather than comply to plan • Plan, deliver, and measure in small batches • Measure business outcomes, not stage outputs • Sense and respond to business conditions • Apply adaptive planning at multiple levels • Conduct strategy planning • Conduct portfolio planning • Conduct product and release planning • Conduct Sprint/iteration and daily planning

Table 1.1. (*continued*)

Agile VMO Function	Responsibilities
Tracking and monitoring program flow	• Understand visual management systems • Track and monitor program flow with visual management systems • Measure and improve flow • Drive continuous learning and adaptation
Prioritizing and selecting minimally marketable products (MMPs)	• Plan for a fundamental shift from project to MMP delivery • Select MMPs for maximum financial impact • Use weighted shortest job first to prioritize and select the most impactful options • Deliver the MMP and learn
Evolving a funding and governance strategy	• Keep your funding model flexible • Provide fixed funding for value streams • Strategize more frequently; annual is not enough • Monetize at the feature level • Devise a fixed-cost model for your stable agile teams • Adopt business outcomes as key governance controls • Utilize a lean business case • Require frequent delivery, and measure incremental business results • Recognize that it is fundamentally about the time value of money
Managing organizational change	• Recognize that change is extraordinarily difficult • Design and set up a holistic change management system • Position the VMO to drive the change

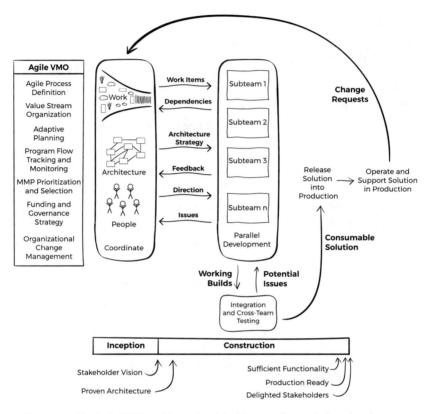

Figure 1.4: *The Agile VMO and Disciplined Agile's team of teams (adapted with permission from PMI)*

In following chapters, learn how to set up an Agile VMO and explore all the fundamental aspects of the VMO's work:

- In chapter 2, understand how to define an agile process at your organization.
- In chapter 3, explore how to reconfigure and organize around value streams.
- In chapter 4, implement adaptive planning at all organizational levels, from the top of your organization down to your agile teams.
- In chapter 5, explore how to use visual management systems and other key techniques to track and monitor program flow.

- In chapter 6, learn to decompose projects and products into smaller increments by prioritizing and selecting MMPs.
- In chapter 7, extend these concepts to business considerations by evolving a funding and governance strategy.
- In chapter 8, consider ways to manage organizational change.
- Finally, in chapter 9, make a detailed plan to set up your own Agile VMO.

To get a flavor of how the VMO has been implemented in industry to achieve business outcomes, see the sidebar for a case study from Nationwide Insurance.[6]

CASE STUDY: IMPLEMENTING THE AGILE VMO AT NATIONWIDE INSURANCE

How has the Agile VMO been implemented in leading organizations? Nationwide Insurance is a Fortune 100 company that has won many accolades over the years. The company has been implementing lean and agile methods since 2007 and had over 230 agile teams, mostly within the information technology department, as of early 2019.

At a 2019 agile industry conference, Nationwide's associate vice president Charles Kennedy presented the following case study. The Enterprise Digital group at Nationwide implemented a VMO with exceptional results: going from a single monthly release to 50 times a month, improving business-side velocity by 67 percent, improving end-to-end cycle time by 30 percent, and reducing costs simultaneously by 15 percent.

Despite advanced agile capability within software development, Nationwide Insurance had an existing "Scrummerfall" approach, as shown in figure 1.5. This antipattern is prevalent across the industry, since most agile adoptions originate within IT and have been driven by CIOs.

At Nationwide, long, linear, upfront planning cycles eventually fed work to agile delivery teams, only to then have the completed work languish in further waterfall steps toward deployment. Nationwide's

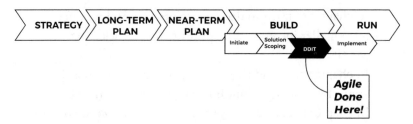

Figure 1.5: *Typical agile-only-in-IT antipattern*

highly visible and competitive digital channels, such as customer-facing websites, mobile apps, and voice channels, required a far more responsive model.

In late 2016, the Nationwide Enterprise Digital group began a business transformation to further improve speed to market and increase flexibility in the highly competitive digital customer-facing channel environment. Nationwide's VMO transformation had three key elements:

- Realigning the organization around value streams as represented by customer journeys, and populating them with end-to-end teams for flow, throughput, and customer outcomes
- Driving collaboration across organizational silos using big room planning to minimize the effect of silos and dependencies
- Prioritizing MMPs to deliver customer value with maximum speed and minimum waste

According to Kennedy, enterprise digital teams partnered across business and IT to successfully pilot an end-to-end model with the Agile VMO that worked directly with end business units and customers. This model then spread organically to other groups within the company.

Summary

The dust is settling on the next normal in our pandemic era. Agile methods have provided a rock-solid foundation on which to grow

Figure 1.6: *Collaboration across silos with big room planning*

and evolve an organization. Organizations can drive business agility in the pandemic era and beyond by understanding true customer needs, learning, and moving faster to produce innovative and in-demand products and services.

As legacy organizations transition to a newer end-to-end agile operating model, the roles of middle management need to unfreeze and not only accept but encourage change. The PMO needs to redesign its mission and operation to be more value adding, less bureaucratic, more customer focused, and more in line with agile product management and other modern ways of working. The PMO must be repurposed toward value management. To accomplish this, the PMO needs to rapidly evolve into an Agile VMO.

Achieving true end-to-end business agility requires transitioning to a new VMO team-of-teams structure and methodical restructuring of processes and structures along our organization's entire value stream.

Try This: Big Room Planning

To begin exploring the VMO team-of-teams model, try out the popular organizational planning technique known as big room planning. This technique is an agile practice that helps multiple teams align and coordinate on business goals and product releases. The essential concept is for everyone involved to congregate in a big room and plan together, as illustrated in figure 1.6. While typically done quarterly, big room planning can also be held on a tighter cadence (e.g., monthly) in fast-moving environments. See chapter 4 for how to prepare for and run an in-person or virtual two-day big room planning event.

2 ■ Defining an Agile Process

Quite often in the early stages of agile adoption, agile teams are able to be successful because they don't have to comply with a lot of burdensome and stifling rules. In fact, using an initial controlled, pilot team approach that is outside of traditional governance is one that has been successful over decades at organizations ranging from Capital One, PayPal, Salesforce, Nike, Spotify, American Express, and the National Geographic Society to the U.S. Library of Congress and the U.S. Department of Homeland Security. If we want to institutionalize agile methods, however, a key job of the Agile VMO is to help develop enterprise-class agile processes and practices that not only support agile delivery but also make them well defined and repeatable.

In particular, many organizations that are publicly traded, highly regulated, or government agencies need to have defined, repeatable, auditable processes and evidence that the processes are being followed. Sadly, in many cases, the vast majority of the work in these types of organizations is still being executed in a traditional water-fall way. Even in 2020, these organizations retained vestiges of industrial-age management. Consequently, many of them have set up PMOs or centers of excellence to drive process standardization and excellence. In the past, these organizations have defined traditional linear processes that are now likely to be too slow, cumbersome, and expensive to be competitive. Misguided organizations will put in so much traditional oversight that they negate all of the benefits that they had hoped for.

Many of these same organizations are now attempting to transition to agile delivery at scale. Some have already been practicing some form of agile development at the team level for some time. Often, the agile work that has been happening has been operating somewhat under the radar from a process controls and audit standpoint. Not surprisingly, this under-the-radar agile work has often been very successful at the team level. Clearly, when you unburden teams from heavy, linear, and bureaucratic overhead and let them work in a more unregulated way they are able to get things done more quickly. This kind of success starts to get some attention. "We should do all of our work this way!" some senior executive might say. So, from the grassroots success comes the desire to scale agile so that more of the work is done in an agile way.

We need to be aware of the dark side when it comes to the organization at large. Even as teams have forged ahead, there has been a spotty application of common agile methods, lack of internal standards, relatively undefined and haphazard processes, confusion around process artifacts or deliverables, and undefined controls and metrics. Across teams, this quickly generates enormously high levels of redundancy, waste, and missed outcomes. As agile processes grow within any organization, the less likely it is that teams will continue to be able to fly under the radar. As large, regulated, audited firms grow their use of agile, they must come to terms with repeatability, auditability, controls, governance, and traceability. Are you seeing a potential problem looming here?

Organizations that seek to practice modern delivery methods need to be both agile and compliant, but achieving both will require significant changes to processes and controls. The challenge then, is to define repeatable and auditable processes that don't actually end up killing the very agility, flexibility, and speed that we are trying to achieve. Known in lean circles as the six sigma paradox, the VMO's challenge is to minimize process variability, slack, and redundancy by building variability, slack, and redundancy into our organizations. That is, we have to create standardized processes and controls at the program and enterprise levels that spur nonstandardized experimentation, risk-taking, and innovation at the team level.

To be successful and to achieve the goals of agile at scale, the VMO will need to instill this form of disciplined agility by doing the following:

- defining agile processes that actually allow or even enforce delivery of value to the organization early and often instead of getting in the way
- shifting the metrics and reporting that are used to measure project effectiveness away from traditional waterfall process-output metrics and toward business-outcome metrics
- changing the controls that are used to govern projects away from phase-based and paper-based artifacts to controls that enforce good agile practices
- creating flexibility in how results are achieved by making experimentation an expected part of the process
- minimizing low-value, high-overhead documentation or artifacts that are not natural outputs of an agile process

Before we dive into our agile processes for product development, let's return to successful COVID-19 responses for a moment. Governments in Mongolia, Vietnam, Ghana, South Korea, and New Zealand acted speedily, with great discipline, and with end-to-end practices like rapid and widespread testing, border closures, contact tracing, prohibition of large public events, and funding of medical equipment and personnel.[1] Their success in controlling the pandemic spread derived in large part from their leaders' alacrity to establish sensible practices and their entire populations following those practices.

Establish High Discipline as the Driving Goal for All Your Agile Processes

To the uninitiated, agile methods can look like an unstructured and undisciplined approach to delivery, but this would be a gross mischaracterization and would also represent a lack of clear understanding. At their core, agile methods have their basis in lean manufacturing and the Toyota production system as conceptualized in figure 2.1. The Toyota production system is the basis for Toyota's amazing success. Toyota reliably and routinely achieves business results that all organizations desire and need:

- high degrees of quality at scale
- high degrees of customer satisfaction
- low internal cost
- consistently high levels of profitability

This consistent level of profitability and quality is one reason why Toyota is one of the most studied organizations in the world. Toyota

Figure 2.1: *The Toyota car factory as a model for lean thinking and continuous flow*

is a model for how lean thinking, continuous flow, and a zero-defect mentality can be a basis for process improvement in almost any business process.

Let's be very clear here. Lean manufacturing is a highly successful, well-tested, scalable, and solid approach to industrial engineering. It is not a set of shortcuts, it is not hacking, and it is not achieved without serious industrial-scale process discipline. Lean's process offspring, including agile product development, can and should be just as disciplined. All agile methods stress this discipline. At the team level, Scrum and Kanban espouse process discipline, just as extreme programming espouses engineering discipline. Other scaling methods, such as LeSS, Disciplined Agile, and SAFe, discussed later, all explicitly call for lean process discipline.

But in many organizations, due to a lack of knowledge, lack of experience, and a lack of clear expectations, agile teams sometimes work without the expected discipline. To many leaders, agile teams may look undisciplined. In some cases, perhaps they are. This is not how it is supposed to be, and it will be difficult to scale without a certain level of discipline. What is really sad is to hear agile team members say things like, "We are agile; we don't have to estimate/plan/document." This shows a clear lack of education and understanding, and it is worrisome that we would entrust millions of dollars in product engineering budget and trust the goodwill of our customers to this misguided thinking. In fact, agile methods have planning and plenty of it, which will be discussed in more detail in chapter 4.

Good agile teams are highly disciplined. Period. It takes a high degree of discipline to deliver working, tested software every two weeks. It is almost impossible to deliver quality software this quickly without it. The most highly disciplined teams that we have seen have been high-functioning agile teams. It is not uncommon for less disciplined teams to be precisely the ones that have difficulty delivering successfully against their commitments. All agile teams need to take a calibrated approach to defining their agile processes.

Take a Calibrated Approach to Defining Your Agile Processes

Agile is itself not a single process, but many processes are deemed to be agile. Defined in 2001 as an umbrella term for all agile processes at that time, the "Manifesto for Agile Software Development" is a set of 4 values and 12 principles that describe the characteristics of good agile development. Here are a few of the principles:

- customer satisfaction by early and continuous delivery of valuable software
- welcome changing requirements, even in late development
- deliver working software frequently (weeks rather than months)
- close, daily cooperation between businesspeople and developers
- working software is the primary measure of progress
- continuous attention to technical excellence and good design[2]

To reiterate, while agile itself is not a single process, many processes are agile, as indicated in figure 2.2, and are designed to achieve these principles. All of the agile approaches—such as Scrum, extreme programming, and Kanban at the team level and SAFe, Scrum at Scale, and Disciplined Agile at the program or portfolio level—can and should be highly disciplined and well executed.

The first step to a calibrated approach is to develop a basic-process road map.

Develop a Basic-Process Road Map

We wouldn't expect a budding musician to play advanced music until years of fundamental skills have been established. However, we often expect teams that are new to agile to have perfect business goals, perfect requirements, perfect estimation, perfect planning, perfect technical practices, perfect communications, and perfect delivery. We expect that all of this be done with blinding speed, right from the beginning. This just isn't going to happen.

Part of the VMO's change strategy will be to lay out a basic agile-process road map with high-level goals and achievable timelines

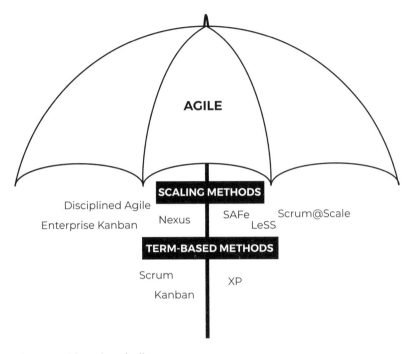

Figure 2.2: *The agile umbrella*

such as those in figure 2.3. For example, we might have a goal that, after the first six months, all teams are practicing all of the basic events and artifacts of Scrum and also have a basic automated smoke test in place. The VMO can then add metrics to see where the organization is in terms of meeting this goal.

Six months later, perhaps we are ready to take on an organizational goal of effective cross-team planning and cross-team integration. Another common management issue is trying to measure too many things too early, thereby loading the teams up with too many competing priorities and goals. Instead, we might plan for new metrics to be put in place only after successful cross-team builds have been established. By working this way, the organization is using metrics to both support and drive the change strategy. Additionally, we are making current goals and process expectations clear to teams.

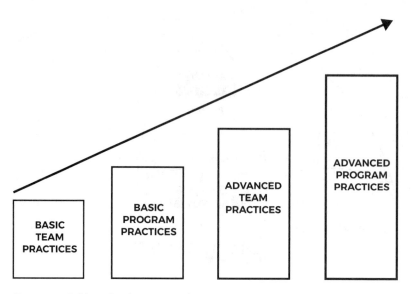

Figure 2.3: *Calibrated agile process road map*

Start with Scrum or Kanban as Your Base Process

In the saying, a journey of a thousand miles begins with a single step. The first step in a multiyear agile journey is to establish a base process, and this is usually Scrum or Kanban or sometimes a hybrid of both, ScrumBan.

Scrum is a well-defined process for new product development. These practices can easily form the basis of a standard agile delivery process for individual teams and even teams of teams. We highlight Scrum because it is by far the most popular of the agile delivery processes and it has a fairly well-understood and accepted set of practices. The Scrum process, as it is commonly practiced, has five events that every team should be practicing and at least four core artifacts that are natural outputs of the process and that each team should be producing. Figure 2.4 and tables 2.1 and 2.2 outline the elements of commonly practiced Scrum.

Scrum seeks to instill a rolling-wave planning cycle where we plan out several weeks of work, execute and deliver that work, then plan the next few weeks. For plannable work, this can be great. However, in many areas, planning even two weeks' worth of work may be al-

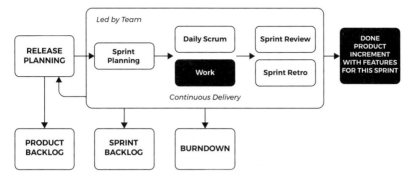

Figure 2.4: *Basic Scrum process*

Table 2.1. *Scrum Events/Ceremonies*

Scrum Event	Description
Release planning	A timeboxed planning session that answers several key questions: What is the goal of the next release, what functionality will be in the release, and when will that release happen? While not a required process step, release planning is commonly performed.
Sprint planning	A short planning session that answers two key questions: What can be achieved in the upcoming Sprint and how can it be achieved?
Sprint	A timebox of one month or less during which a done, usable, and potentially releasable product increment is created.
Daily Scrum	A daily 15-minute event, also called stand-up, for the team to synchronize activities and create a plan for the next 24 hours.
Sprint review	Is held at the end of the Sprint to inspect the product increment and adjust the product backlog if needed.
Sprint retrospective	Happens after the Sprint review and addresses what went well during the Sprint, what could be improved, and what the team will commit to improve in the next Sprint.

Table 2.2. *Scrum Artifacts*

Scrum Artifact	Description
Product backlog	An ordered list of everything that is known to be needed in the product. It is the single source of requirements.
Sprint backlog	The set of product backlog items selected for the Sprint. It makes visible all the work that the team needs to meet the Sprint goal. The backlog has enough detail that changes in progress can be understood on a daily basis in the daily scrum.
Burndown chart	A chart showing the number of stories or points still remaining to be completed within the Sprint.
Product increment	A body of inspectable work. The increment must be usable by customers. The entire point of scrum is to deliver a done increment.

most impossible. A prime example is operational support. In the support world, planning can be extraordinarily difficult because we don't know what is going to break tomorrow, how impactful the breakage will be, or how complex the solution will be. Support is often a very reactive function. The problem for us as leaders then is: How can we manage the unplannable?

Another agile method that is quite popular for operational work is Kanban. Kanban is interrupt driven and is the obvious choice for operational work and also most work that is not new product development. In Kanban, we don't lock the scope for even two weeks. Instead, we continuously reprioritize the work as it comes in. Our product owner sets priorities from day to day or even hour to hour and the team simply pulls the highest item off the list and works on it until done. We also impose work-in-progress (WIP) limits to prevent the team from working on too many items at once. By focusing on just a few top priority items at once, the team can achieve a continuous flow of delivery that is very reactive to the latest changing priorities. This does not mean that Kanban cannot be used for plannable work; it certainly can be. Likewise, Scrum, with some modifications, can be used to manage unplannable work too. Scrum is used more frequently for plannable work, and Kanban is used more frequently for unplannable work. Kanban sounds easy and simple, but having the discipline to do it well is in fact quite difficult. It requires extraordinary discipline.

Teams that say that they are doing Scrum should be able to demonstrate evidence of each of the previously mentioned events and artifacts in every Sprint. VMOs can start to help their organizations achieve consistency and repeatability by setting expectations that these very simple and natural outcomes of the Scrum process are expected from all Scrum teams. Likewise, Kanban teams should be able to show that they have a clearly prioritized backlog, have and adhere to WIP limits, have flow metrics, and perhaps have classes of delivery and can demonstrate a continuous flow of delivery.

From a process standpoint, there is nothing here that the vast majority of experienced people in the agile community should complain about, and this simple list of process controls is an adequate way to start putting discipline around agile delivery teams. These simple rules create the foundation for strong process discipline, create the foundation for organizational agility, and minimize nonagile overhead. At the same time, we need to remove legacy process controls that do not contribute to or encourage agility, such as the following:

- Most waterfall phase gates and reviews such as design reviews, architecture reviews, and security reviews. Review these frequently and iteratively instead.
- Heavy up-front documentation. We should go lightweight instead. Small, frequent deployments should require only small amounts of paperwork.

Scrum and Kanban are integral to all scaling methods and are the foundations on which all enterprise agile transformations should be built.

Take a Focused, Minimalist Approach to Scaling
When all of our individual teams operate with a relatively simple but powerful level of Scrum or Kanban discipline, we can begin to scale multiple teams in order to support larger and more complex efforts. When we scale, we combine the efforts of many teams into a single, larger endeavor or program. In these cases, the estimates, plans, and approaches that each team uses must somehow integrate well with the approaches that other teams are using. Beyond the individual team goals and plans, there need to be program- or product-level goals, plans, estimates, and schedules.

Larger agile programs need another level of process events and artifacts that integrate the efforts of the individual teams. This will add yet another layer of estimation, planning, and reporting, and it is difficult if not impossible to avoid this. Luckily, scaling methods, including the Scaled Agile Framework (SAFe) and Disciplined Agile, provide reasonably holistic ways to deal with both team level and program level planning and management. The several scaling approaches available have many common elements. Some elements common to all scaling methods are outlined in figure 2.5

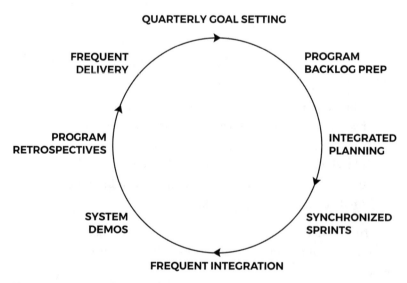

Figure 2.5: *Common elements of agile at scale*

Despite their commonalities, each scaling method is unique in some way to large-scale planning, delivery, integration, and reporting. Whichever scaling method we select, the VMO helps define clear program-level process expectations for scaled agile practices such as the following:

o multiteam planning events
o frequent multiteam integration and demos
o frequent multiteam scrum of scrums
o regular program-wide retrospectives
o demand versus capacity planning
o work-item prioritization based on weighted shortest job first
o clear, measurable business goals that are achievable in the near term
o visible work management system—that is, program Kanban
o plans that map stories or features for each team for the next several Sprints
o release burndown/burnup by feature
o program-level Sprint-over-Sprint velocity

No matter which scaling methodology we select, the same advice applies: if we want our teams to do good SAFe or good Disciplined Agile, then we should set clear expectations and not make them spend time on unnecessary activities that could be spent on the respective process. It's really quite simple: do the agile process of your choice, do it very well, and minimize the time spent doing anything else.

Define Metrics That Support and Drive Dynamic Transformation

Another key area of focus for the VMO is metrics. Metrics have a big role in driving human behavior. Appropriate selection of metrics is therefore critical to agile transformation and execution to move us in the right direction. Metrics bring strong focus to process, to outcomes, and ultimately to behaviors. Chosen correctly, metrics will foster and accelerate agility. Chosen poorly, metrics will enforce the wrong process, the wrong outcomes, and the wrong behaviors. Many organizations make the classic mistake of trying to change the process while keeping the same metrics that they had previously in the hope that the new process will improve the old metrics. This is almost certainly doomed to fail. You may have heard that "What gets measured gets managed." A corollary to this might be that you can't manage if you are measuring the wrong thing. We will discuss some metrics that are appropriate for agile programs in more detail later.

Metrics should not remain static. We want the goals and challenges that we have early in our agile transformation to be different from the issues and goals that we have two years from now.

For example, early on in the agile journey, we often have problems just getting teams to perform good agile practices and helping them to better manage work in progress. It will be difficult to scale until we can get these basics under control. Later, as we scale, the challenges may move to those related to reliable integration, thorough system testing, dependency management, and business outcome measurement. Perhaps we are having technical issues around balancing quality and reliability, and so there may be a focus on DevOps technical practices which might drive another set of metrics. The point is that our challenges and goals will change over time, and the key metrics that we track should change also.

Balance Business and Information Technology Metrics

VMO leaders should measure both business and delivery metrics. In general, there is way too much focus on schedule and cost estimates, delivery metrics, and compliance metrics and not nearly enough focus on business value metrics (see figure 2.6). Many large, expensive programs are way overburdened with delivery metrics but have no business outcome metrics. Measurements of feature usage, customer satisfaction, program profitability, customer retention, and feature-level return on investment are scant if they even exist at all. Neglecting these business metrics leads to questionable investments and investment performance management at best and hampers busi-

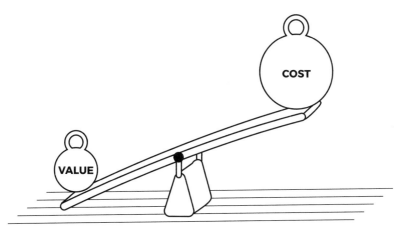

Figure 2.6: *Balance value and cost*

ness agility. We will discuss this topic in more detail in chapter 7, but for now, the message is that we need just as much focus on business-side value metrics as there is on delivery metrics

Unfortunately, business results or outcome metrics are lagging indicators in that they do not provide any measurement of success until after delivery happens. This feedback occurs way too late to be useful on traditional waterfall programs, because by the time we get the feedback, the program is over. However, there is one important way that the VMO should address the lagging indicator problem on agile programs: deliver early, deliver often, and measure business results repeatedly.

Using agile, we should be able to deliver something of value to a customer early and start to get fast and useful feedback as shown in figure 2.7. We do this over and over again and use that feedback to make each incremental release of the product better and better. *Better* can mean many things: increased customer usability, enhanced functionality, simplified functionality, and improved internal business results. Many organizations have a very misguided approach to agile in that they do not require that their programs deliver to production frequently enough. They go through many Sprints of development and try to maintain a single release near the end. This is basically just waterfall development and little more.

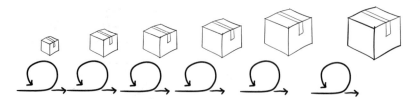

Figure 2.7: *Incremental delivery*

Agile is a feedback-based system, and the most reliable feedback is from real users, not from internal people who claim to speak on behalf of customers. To be agile, you need to deliver early and get the feedback, and the VMO should enforce this through governance and controls. In this regard, actual delivery metrics are critical. VMOs should measure how long it is before programs deliver their first release and how frequently they release. If there are no releases, then we simply aren't doing agile.

That should take care of the lagging indicator issue to a great extent. That said, there are some leading indicators that can be measured during these short development cycles that might have value in predicting the likelihood of early delivery and of quality.

The classic Sprint and release burndown charts are great indicators of basic progress against scope and schedule (figure 2.8). Simply, a burndown chart shows what remains, while a burnup chart shows what has been done. The Sprint burndown gives an indication of short-term schedule performance. The release burnup gives an indication of longer-term schedule performance. They are both beautiful in their simplicity, yet sadly, many so-called agile teams neglect to produce them.

Sprint velocity is another simple and powerful metric that tries to show how predictable our teams are. Sprint-over-Sprint comparison of planned versus actual delivery measures what the teams estimated that they could get done versus what they actually got done, Sprint by Sprint, as shown in figure 2.9. Ideally, we'd like our teams to eventually get pretty good at being able to plan out what they can get done. The reality in many organizations, however, is that sometimes they get a lot done and sometimes they get zero done.

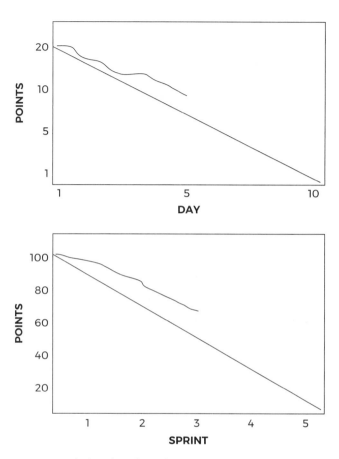

Figure 2.8: *Sprint and release burndown charts*

Problems can arise when teams have highly unpredictable delivery. It is hard to hit a planned delivery date when teams cannot reliably predict their velocity. Oftentimes, the issues are not the team's fault. Just because a team cannot deliver what they planned does not mean the team is underperforming. There are often environment issues, data issues, network issues, team members getting pulled out to do other work, constant changes in priority, teams being asked to juggle three different efforts at the same time, and other things outside of their control that are causing the problems. Agile methods are fantastic for finding and highlighting all of the issues that keep us from delivering.

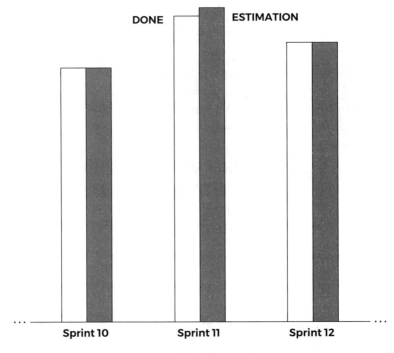

Figure 2.9: *Estimation versus done in Sprint-by-Sprint comparison*

Look for Patterns in the Metrics across Teams

Individual teams and their scrum masters and product owners will need to review their own data and develop action plans for continuous improvement. The VMO, however, should look a level up from the individual team metrics and try to uncover organizational patterns that are impacting multiple teams. If there are just a few teams that are struggling, then those particular teams may need attention and focus. In our experience, we usually see the opposite: most of the teams are struggling to deliver. If there are many teams that are unable to meet commitments, are experiencing serious issues, or have unpredictable delivery, then the problems are not with the teams themselves. When many teams experience challenges, this is a clear sign that larger organizational issues outside of any one team's span of control are at play. Basically, leadership and management issues are not being adequately addressed.

Unfortunately, in many projectized organizations, there is no ownership of issues outside of individual teams or projects. There is often nobody who has clear ownership of how all projects interact with each other or how shared services and central financial systems and information security are supposed to integrate with a hundred different agile teams. The VMO should use the data that is coming in from the teams to try to uncover the larger issues that need higher levels of leadership to solve. Perhaps there are environment issues, database issues, tooling inadequacies, capacity issues, or other factors that are outside of any individual team's ability to solve. This is one big area where the VMO can provide immense value: by addressing the systemic issues that keep the organization as a whole from being able to deliver.

Keep Metrics Simple and Small in Number

Table 2.3 has some sample metrics that some organizations use to measure agility at the team, program, and business level. These may be appropriate for an organization that is early in its agile maturity; more mature organizations may be ready to move on to the next level of performance metrics. Note that these are just a sample and your VMO should put significant thought into developing a small number of impactful metrics that will drive the kinds of specific behaviors and maturity that your organization needs in this particular moment.

Develop Process Controls as Natural Outputs of the Process

To have an auditable process, we need to have a defined process and clear evidence that it is being closely followed. This has an important corollary that VMOs are well advised to understand. Any activities that are required that are not a natural part of the agile process will take time away from the actual execution of the agile process. If you want teams to do good Scrum, then don't make them spend tons of time doing things that aren't Scrum.

For example, good agile teams will often develop big visible-information radiators that make plans and status and goals and

Table 2.3. *Sample Metrics by Area*

Metric Area	Sample Metrics
Business metrics	Capture intended versus actual business outcome metrics per release or per quarter. These are the most important metrics but are often the most lacking. Examples include • account sign-ups • reduced help-desk calls • improved customer satisfaction surveys • improved customer retention • growth in application usage
Program metrics	• Number of integrations and system demos. It is only by integrating early and often, and by demoing the full system, that we can really know where we truly are in terms of progress and quality. All other interim metrics are guesses at best. • Feature-level progress. Features for the upcoming release will often be broken down into several lower-level user stories, and it can be advantageous to track how much of the planned feature is being delivered versus what was planned. This indicates the completeness of the feature. • Release burnup chart. Shows the cumulative point value of user stories planned for the release that are done as a function of time. By looking at this chart, we can estimate how much of the overall cumulative planned work for the release will be done by the planned release date. This indicates the completeness of the release versus what was planned.
Team metrics	• Points planned versus points delivered by Sprint in order to assess predictability • Sprint burndown to assess short-term schedule performance • Release burnup to assess long-term schedule performance • Mixture of work item types to measure how much of the team's time is being applied to new-value delivery versus defect fixing or maintenance

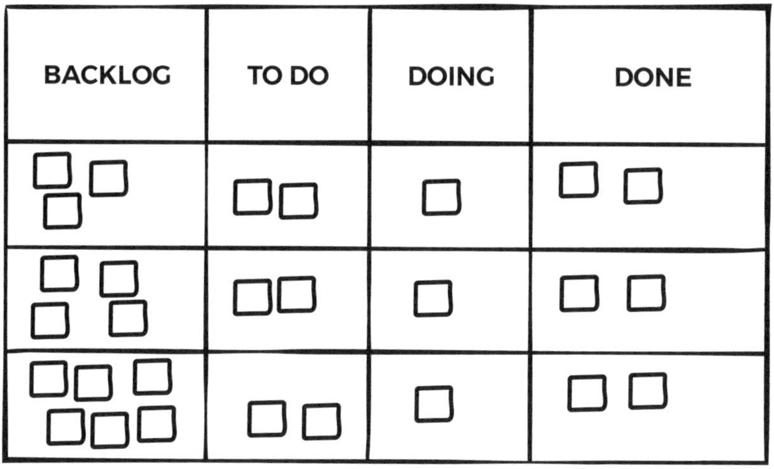

Figure 2.10: *Information radiator*

priorities easily visible to all, as illustrated in figure 2.10. Taking a photo of team walls and regularly posting it to an internal wiki could potentially serve as evidence that the process is being followed without having to resort to creating time-consuming and soul-sapping documents that few are likely to ever read. By the 2020s pandemic age, most of us have transitioned to working from home and are using digital boards in tools like Jira. This has made process compliance easier, since all artifacts and reports are available in the tools themselves. Simple process controls such as these are not onerous or draconian or bureaucratic; quite simply, they are natural outcomes of good and disciplined execution of well-accepted agile process.

Embed Controls at Multiple Process Levels

As we scale agile to larger efforts with the approach we've laid out, we will have several levels of process discipline and controls. There are the team-level expectations that we discussed earlier. On top of that, we will likely need program-level controls to help manage the integrated efforts of many teams. And then portfolio-level controls are needed to effectively manage the overall flow of work through a larger organization. Once again, at each level, the controls should be natural outcomes of the agile process chosen. Table 2.4. is an

Table 2.4. *Process Controls at Multiple Levels*

Organizational Level	Sample Controls

Team-level process controls	• High-level features or epics are captured in an approved agile work management tool.
	• All lower-level user stories, defects, and other work items are captured in the tool and are tied back to the appropriate higher-level feature or epic.
	• Backlog items that are targeted for the current release are estimated in points.
	• The team produces Sprint burndown charts and release burnup charts.
	• The team tracks Sprint-over-Sprint velocity to measure predictability.
	• The team has demonstrated practice of at least the following events:
	  ○ Release planning
	  ○ Sprint planning
	  ○ Daily stand-ups
	  ○ Sprint reviews
	  ○ Sprint retrospectives

Program-level process controls	The following program-level controls list assumes that a SAFe framework is being used. A slightly different but similar list should be created for organizations that are adopting Project Management Institute's Disciplined Agile, Scrum at Scale, or other scaling mechanism. For example, an organization practicing SAFe might have expectations such as these: • A visible program Kanban that implements the work intake and approval funnel • Weighted-shortest-job-first scores that justify the work for the coming quarter • Early and frequent release of value to customers • Measured business results from each release

Table 2.4. (*continued*)

Organizational Level	Sample Controls

	• Program increment planning events that occur at least quarterly with all teams and dependencies and product owners in attendance
	• System integration demos that occur at least quarterly
	• Inspect and adapt workshops that occur at least quarterly
	• Program increment planning outputs that result in
	   ○ Sprint plans for every team for the next quarter's worth of Sprints
	   ○ stories that are estimated and put into targeted Sprints
	   ○ dependencies across teams that are captured
	   ○ risks are identified and a risk management plan is in place

Portfolio-level process controls	• All major investment requests have a lightweight business case that includes measurable business outcome objectives. • There is a clear and agreed-to way that the business outcomes will be measured. • Projects/programs are not weighed or considered independently. Instead, all new work requests are brought to the table at regular intervals and must compete against each other. • Projects/program work in progress is limited to available capacity; teams and individuals are not expected to support more than two simultaneous efforts, and there is strong preference for only one effort per team at a time. • The portfolio is visualized in a centralized location so that there is broad transparency into the number of simultaneous programs and the progress of each. • Business outcomes are openly reviewed and measured quarterly. • Objective, measurable business outcomes are the primary measurement used to justify continued funding.

example set of process controls at the team, program, and portfolio levels that are fairly consistent with most approaches to agile delivery. These can easily be tailored depending on your organization's required level of audit and compliance rigor.

Table 2.4 is just a sample of some of the key controls that your VMO will need to put in place in order to create an agile organization. These controls are all fairly natural outcomes of an organization that is operating using lean and agile principles. By this, we mean that these controls are organic to the process itself and that no additional documents or artifacts have been added simply because we've always done them or because they have been commonplace in the past.

Define Team-Level Agile Process Expectations

In talking with many teams over the years, we often hear that no clear expectations have been put in place around agile development and so they are left to define the process and the inputs and the outputs themselves. Naturally this leads to a significant amount of confusion and variation. In these organizations, no two agile teams operate the same way, few if any have a well-understood basic set of process steps, they often lack metrics, and they often skip key parts of the process such as continuous improvement or customer demos. Naturally, with not even basic standards in place, product development can often be somewhat chaotic. Note that this approach can and often does work at the individual team level. Small teams working on relatively small efforts that have minimal external dependencies may be able to work this way very successfully, but it is impossible to scale this level of variation across many teams without redundancy, waste, and misalignment between teams. It will also be difficult to use this sort of agile development to deliver large complex products. What works in a small team of 10 people with a few engineers and others who are creating a relatively small product will not likely work when you try to scale it up to hundreds or even thousands who are creating a power-plant control system, a satellite communications system, advanced embedded medical electronics, or financial trading systems that move billions of dollars. In addition, this level of variability likely will not meet the expectations for process definition and repeatability that most large organizations must be able to show. A basic level of process discipline is absolutely essential to create a larger agile organization. Watch out, though, because it is all too easy to kill agility with unnecessary overhead.

Define Program- and Portfolio-Level Agile Process Expectations

Similarly, multiple teams working at the program or portfolio levels should have clear expectations on what is required to pull the efforts of multiple teams together. Without strong coordination, each team can easily go in its own direction in terms of design decisions, user interface patterns, security, database access, and more. This can lead to some chaos where each team is meeting its individual goals but we are missing the attainment of a coherent, integrated system. To keep this from happening, we will need program-level expectations such as some of the following:

- frequent system builds, integration, testing, and demonstration
- forward planning sessions around dependency discovery, planning, and management
- architecture and design working groups who collaboratively decide and document how common technical issues will be handled
- program-wide retrospectives to improve coordination, planning, communications, and integration
- Scrum-of-scrums meetings where leaders from each team get together to jointly address challenges
- product-owner working groups that prioritize work for the program in a coherent way that results in useful functionality for the end user

The controls and process expectations needn't be heavy or document rich. They do need to act as frequent checkpoints that constantly bring the teams back together again and work toward a single common system that doesn't look and behave like it was created by 10 different teams.

Protect Delivery Teams from Bureaucracy

A fine balance is required if we are to be both disciplined and successful in achieving organizational agility. Teams cannot deliver valuable working software to customers if they are saddled with low-value, bureaucratic compliance overhead that detracts from their mission of delivery value to customers. The VMO must protect teams from this common issue. How can the VMO both protect teams from low-value process overhead while still achieving the high degrees of discipline needed to ship high-quality software early and often and have it done in ways that are defined and auditable? The answer is actually very simple: **define what is meant by *agile*, set high expectations for teams to execute agile processes very well**, and **shield them from having to do anything that isn't a normal part of generally accepted agile practices**.

By working in this way, we achieve a well-defined process, a high degree of process excellence and repeatability, and a more agile organization.

CASE STUDY: PROCESS DEFINITION AT THE U.S. CITIZENSHIP AND IMMIGRATION SERVICES

The U.S. Citizenship and Immigration Services within the U.S. Department of Homeland Security is an amazing case study in large-scale organizational agility.[3] The results of their agile adoption have been astounding, going from average release frequency of approximately every 180 days down to two weeks or less for most programs. Citizenship and Immigration Services started by developing a relatively simple process model that called for all teams to implement a handful of basic practices such as timeboxed iterations, continuous testing, iteration reviews, and retrospectives. The initial practices are marked by asterisks (*) in figure 2.11. Once a basic implementation of agile delivery had taken hold, they successively added additional process practices. These more

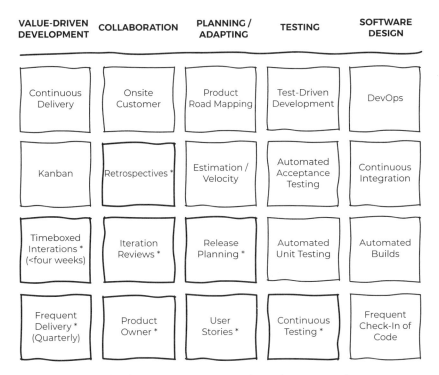

VALUE-DRIVEN DEVELOPMENT	COLLABORATION	PLANNING / ADAPTING	TESTING	SOFTWARE DESIGN
Continuous Delivery	Onsite Customer	Product Road Mapping	Test-Driven Development	DevOps
Kanban	Retrospectives *	Estimation / Velocity	Automated Acceptance Testing	Continuous Integration
Timeboxed Interations * (<four weeks)	Iteration Reviews *	Release Planning *	Automated Unit Testing	Automated Builds
Frequent Delivery * (Quarterly)	Product Owner *	User Stories *	Continuous Testing *	Frequent Check-In of Code

Figure 2.11: *Initial agile practices at U.S. Citizenship and Immigration Services*

advanced practices allowed the organization to mature and become successively more sophisticated in its adoption of agile.

Summary

Scaling agility is difficult if not impossible without a certain level of process discipline. Agile methods allow us to move purposefully fast, and the faster we go, the more disciplined we need to be about our timing and practices. As we scale agility within our organizations, we reach a tipping point at which we are no longer able to fly under the radar and need to have a more defined, repeatable, and auditable agile process. The trick is to not overburden our processes with so much overhead that we lose the very agility that we seek. The key to scaling success is to maximize the extent to which we execute

natural agile practices and minimize the extent to which we do anything that is not agile.

If our organization is going to scrum, then we should do scrum,
do all of it, do it very well, and try to minimize the time that teams
spend doing anything that isn't scrum. Ditto for SAFe, Scrum at
Scale, Nexus, Enterprise Kanban, or whatever framework we choose.
Each of these frameworks comes with a natural set of process controls that will be organic outputs and outcomes of the process. Grav-
itate to these as your control points and standardize on these as
ways to achieve both agility and compliance without excessive process overhead:

- Set firm process expectations that are grounded in a
  commonly accepted team-based or scaled agile approach.
- Do what the process frameworks call for, do it very well,
  and minimize any time doing process-related work that is
  not called for by the framework.
- Set expectations at multiple levels: team, program, and
  portfolio.
- Don't expect to be great at everything right from the start.
  Choose a few practices to focus on at each level, and then
  add more advanced practices as the organization matures
  in its understanding of agile.
- Select a small number of metrics at the team, program,
  and business levels. Choose metrics that are focused on
  solving the problems that you are having today. Then later,
  when you have made progress on these problems, change
  the metrics to address the latest issues. In this way, you
  will have a measurement system that is relevant and useful
  for where your organization is right now.
- Combine the metrics to support a simple organizational
  change road map that takes you to higher and higher levels
  of agility. Use three levels of metrics to get a holistic view:
  business metrics, program metrics, and team metrics.
- Finally, focus on metrics patterns across teams. If many
  teams are struggling, the problem isn't the teams, it is the

organization in which they are trying to operate. Focus your energies on improving the organizational environment so that teams are working in a place where they can be successful. If many teams are unable to meet their objectives, then systemic issues in your organization likely are preventing most teams from getting work done. Get those addressed!

Try This: Basic Agile Practices

Define basic agile practices at the team and program levels. As a first step, lay out a basic agile process road map with high-level goals and achievable time-lines (refer to figure 2.2). Don't try to get too advanced too soon and set expectations that the basics be done well. Set a target goal post for six months, and be sure to put in metrics for the goal to be able to measure progress.

3 ■ Organizing around Value Streams

Nine departmental silos. In our experience, that's the average number of silos that need to be traversed to deliver value to customers in any large organization today. Midsize and even small organizations are not exempt—most operate with silo thinking as their default. Is this your experience as well? If so, we can agree that this is a major, and likely an existential, problem.

The siloed organizational structure may appear efficient to those inside the organization, but it is generally a disaster from a customer's standpoint. Almost anything that a customer needs is likely to require the coordination of many of these siloed functions, each of which often has its own interests and budgets. Consequently, it is either very difficult or sometimes impossible to achieve fast flow of value to the customer. Even just measuring end-to-end flow as a first step toward identifying the bottlenecks impeding flow is very challenging. Things get worse when an organization has a command-and-control, top-down hierarchy. The need to get things done by a throw-it-over-the-wall transfer from silo to silo is compounded by the need to traverse up-and-down organizational totem poles several times to get decisions. Essentially, slow lead time between silos and slow decision velocity across hierarchical layers create rigid organizations. Such organizations have struggled to develop the flexibility needed to survive in a fast-moving modern world and most will likely cease to exist in the pandemic era.

So what can be done quickly? One of the first steps toward breaking down organizational silos like these is to have business and information technology (IT) partners regularly connect with each other. For instance, a banking client of ours needed to set up an omnichannel organization for better end-to-end customer service and innovation. Their first step was to set up a consolidated unit that brought together business partners with agile teams that had hitherto been siloed in the IT organization. After initial and understandable agitation, this unit gelled into a larger, unified team of teams. Another client of ours had taken a similar approach, augmenting a business unit that was very conversant with Lean Six Sigma techniques with agile teams. Quite often a restructuring of the organizational structure is required to get things moving powerfully in the right direction. Of course, any organizational restructuring needs to be thoughtfully designed to be in line with agile principles and executed carefully under executive direction and oversight.

Longer term, what are the types of organizational structures that best support, enable, and grow agile methods? Things get very hairy when the agile notion of small, cross-functional, self-disciplined teams is introduced into our legacy organizations, as illustrated in figure 3.1. Rooted in the manufacturing efficiency mindset from the 1900s, the vast majority of firms worldwide are organized around functional specialties like marketing, finance, sales, and IT. Functional silos that mirror industrial-age production lines are also perpetuated within departments. For instance, within IT, a plethora of subspecialties form the typical basis of organization: requirements analysis, front-end software development, database development, database administration, network engineering, information security, and so on.

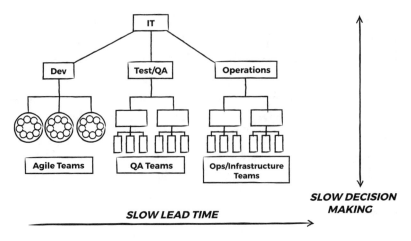

Figure 3.1: *Agile teams in a legacy organizational structure*

Even if we can stand up teams that meet Scrum's guidelines for a cross-functional team of three to nine people with a scrum master and a product owner, we run into misalignment issues, some of which are captured in table 3.1.

If our older industrial-age organizational models are clearly mismatched for agile teams and methods, what are the more suitable alternatives in our current era?

Organize as Adaptive Networks of Teams

In recent years, a modern-day alternative to the industrial-age manufacturing-based organizational model has emerged and is gaining widespread popularity: the understanding of *organizations as adaptive networks of teams organized around specific goals*. Agile methods have long posited that small, cross-functional teams are the natural way for humans to work and to achieve high levels of team productivity and performance. Connecting these high-performance teams into adaptive networks of teams allows individuals and teams to share information and learning transparently across the enterprise and thus adapt quickly and dynamically to change.

Table 3.1. *Organizational Misalignment with Agile Methods*

• While agile methods call for small, cross-functional teams (3–9 people for Scrum), average team size devolves over time to 25+ people.
• While agile methods call for integrated teams with all necessary disciplines represented on the core team, testers get pulled out of the formerly fully integrated team core, and end up in a separate quality assurance silo.
• While agile methods call for team allocation of 80 percent or more for the core team to a single effort, team members end up multitasking on two to three projects at a time.
• While agile methods call for locking down scope within a Sprint/iteration, untrained product owners introduce new user stories while Sprints/iterations are underway.
• While agile methods call for accepting responsibility and team members handling work assignments among themselves, newly hired project managers end up assigning work to team members in Sprint/iteration planning meetings.
• While agile methods call for daily stand-up meetings to be run by the team, they eventually devolve into status meetings for the project managers.

As shown in figure 3.2, networks of teams can be formed and reformed dynamically into different constellations to meet the business goals at hand. This flexible networked model assumes change is normal and is qualitatively different from the traditional linear, mechanistic organizational model that assumes stability is the norm.

From the ground up, there is a clear recognition that each team or organizational component in the network has an impact on every other part as impacts ripple through the larger network. These teams of teams are thus set up so that people work together end to end across the entire organization to *optimize the whole* in response to changing business conditions. Optimizing the whole value stream from the customer's standpoint is a core tenet of lean thinking

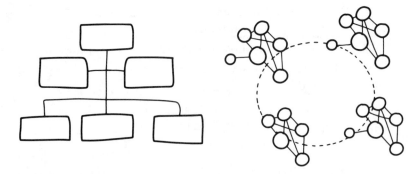

Figure 3.2: *From the industrial to a networked organizational model*

and one that our VMOs should apply in figuring out how to evolve organization models away from the hierarchical and siloed model.

How should we handle scaling up from one team to networks of agile teams? How can we ensure that those networks of teams can be aligned with our business and configured and reconfigured dy-

---

W. L. Gore Network of Teams

W. L. Gore has a long history of product innovation ranging from heart patches to dental floss and guitar strings. This outstanding success is largely credited to its *lattice* organizational structure. With the goal of connecting all individuals in the company to each other, W. L Gore's interconnected lattice organizational structure has the following features:

- A flat hierarchy without formal ranks and title
- Multidisciplinary teams that organize dynamically around business endeavors
- Leaders that emerge on the basis of business needs

In particular, at W. L. Gore scaling is handled in a unique way. Through trial and error, W. L Gore found that divisions tended not to work as a team once they exceeded around 200 associates, and a division-size constraint was established. When divisions begin to grow beyond this limit of 200 people, a new division is launched, with its own 200-person constraint.

These divisions are clustered around business needs in geographical proximity. W. L. Gore has scaled this model successfully over the past 60 years as it has grown revenues to over $3 billion, with over 9000 people in over 30 countries.

namically? One of the most durable examples comes from W. L. Gore and Associates, best known for its GORE-TEX fabric developed originally for rainwear, see sidebar.

Within our organizations, one way we can deploy this network-of-teams model is by using the agile release train technique from SAFe. Multiple teams can be aggregated into an agile release train constellation, as shown in figure 3.3.

In the SAFe, agile release trains range from 50 to 125 people, with the upper limit based on Dunbar's number. The anthropologist Robert Dunbar proposed that 150 is the cognitive limit to the number of people with whom we can maintain stable social relationships.[1] Other anthropologists have put that cognitive limit closer to 300 people. As we look for ways to group teams into larger teams of teams, and those teams of teams into larger constellations, it is useful to consider how best to use this knowledge about cognitive limits to set group size limits at each level. Using guidelines as input into a scaling approach, we can set up the following:

- agile teams that range in size from 3 to 10 people
- multiple teams configured into agile release trains of 50–150 people
- multiple agile release trains configured into constellations with no more than 500 people

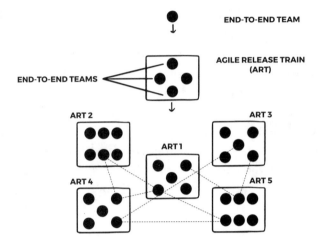

Figure 3.3: *Scaling to multiple teams*

Define Flexible Value Streams by Customer Journeys

Practically, how should one go about implementing the desirable adaptive network-of-teams concept in a modern business or other organization? Successful agile organizations tend to organize their team constellations around the customer in order to provide fast and frictionless cross-functional support and delivery of products or services. A *value stream* is the set of steps that are needed to provide continuous value to our customers. Organizing around the customer using a value stream approach implies the following:

- understanding the primary experiences, journeys, or touch points that customers have with the organization
- creating internal companies within a company that are organized into value streams that directly support these customer experiences
- creating flexible roles and responsibilities that allow these experience-aligned value streams to operate in a more entrepreneurial fashion
- allocating budgets in ways that support the customer value stream from end to end and that are aligned with strategic outcomes

Since we want and expect our VMO to be tasked with team formation and resource allocation, we need new ways of thinking about how to implement these concepts for more effective value delivery and true business agility. Fundamentally, we recommend a two-step approach.

First, evolve from project to product with experience-aligned teams. Second, assign work to teams, not individuals, to ensure alignment within teams.

These steps are covered in detail next.

Evolve from Project to Product with Experience-Aligned Teams

The idea of shifting the underlying organizational structure and processes of an organization from supporting projects to supporting products has been percolating for a while. The core idea is to ensure that the way we fund our work and the ways we organize our teams and organizations enable rapid response to user feedback and changing market conditions.

With a product model, rather than locking ourselves into a brittle organizational structure, our organizational design goal is to set up stable, cross-functional teams that are aligned around a customer experience in a flexible constellation. Rather than allocating team members across multiple projects simultaneously, our cross-functional teams focus on a single minimally marketable product (MMP) at a time. An MMP is a deployable set of minimum product features that address our customers' immediate needs, that deliver value back to our business, and that allow us to test and learn. MMPs allow us to test our assumptions about our markets and customers and learn directly from the results we get from those tests. Figure 3.4 illustrates a basic model for creating an end-to-end team that is experience aligned.

In our example model, each experience-aligned end-to-end team is aligned with and focused on customer experiences like *seamless delivery*, *flexible viewing channels*, and *effortless point of sale*. Replacing the siloed organizational structure, each experience-aligned end-to-end team is set up with all or most of the functions necessary to deliver

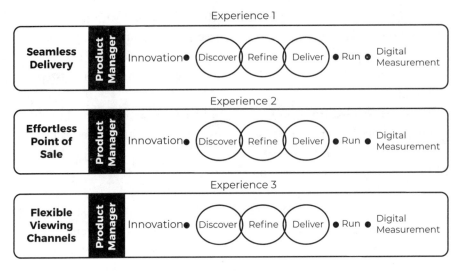

Figure 3.4: *Experience-aligned, end-to-end team model*

value from end to end within the organization to end users. Each team has several types of roles:

- product management, with product owners led by a product manager
- user experience experts, assisting product management with customer discovery activities
- team members conducting innovation experiments through direct end-user contact and prototyping
- other cross-functional members working on MMPs and systematically and progressively breaking them down into epics, features, and user stories in an overlapping discovery-refinement-delivery process
- team members with expertise in production or run activities
- team members focused on digital measurement support

This design helps implement what is known as an inverse Conway maneuver, and in addition to enabling end-to-end communication, it helps us eventually overcome issues with monolithic systems. Recall from chapter 1 Conway's law, which famously states, "Any organization that designs a system (defined broadly) will produce a design whose structure is a copy of the organization's communication structure."[2]

Since we are solving for business agility, this inverse Conway approach evolves our team and organizational structure to promote our desired architecture. That is, we build our teams for flow and that in turn promotes a modern, decoupled architecture. There are several distinct advantages to decoupling teams from one another with this approach. It significantly reduces the cognitive load on each team, as well as the dependencies between teams. Finally, by building our team in a customer experience-aligned constellation, it ensures that our systems and flow of value will also be customer-experience aligned and flexible.

Assign Work to Teams, Not Individuals, to Ensure Alignment within Teams
There are manifold benefits to giving talented team members more autonomy. From a humanistic perspective, people really appreciate having control over how their jobs are done. The more autonomy, the greater their job satisfaction, their sense of well-being, and their overall work engagement.[3] From a financial perspective, better work engagement drives higher productivity, lower costs, and greater value to customers. There is, however, a dark side to superficially increasing individual autonomy without understanding what changes need to be made systemically. In less mature agile organizations, efforts to increase autonomy among team members have counterproductive effects because they are not aligned with each other and not accountable to a larger organizational goal. In mature agile organizations, there is an understanding that autonomy, alignment, and accountability have to go hand in hand. As Kent Beck, the creator of extreme programming, has declared, "Autonomy without accountability is just vacation."[4]

How do we create autonomy for our team members and also ensure they stay aligned and accountable for delivering on organizational goals and customer value? The answer is to first ensure we have experience-aligned end-to-end teams and then to assign work to our experience-aligned teams, and not individuals, as illustrated in figure 3.5.

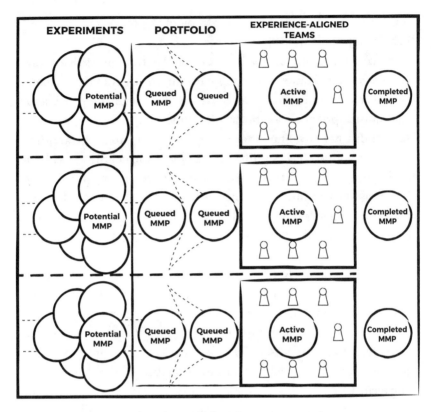

Figure 3.5: *Assigning work to experience-aligned teams*

In this model, prioritized work flows from customer-facing experiments to a portfolio where work is queued for an experience-aligned team. Customer-facing experiments facilitate value discovery and allow us to go from business idea to initial identification of epics in a structured and disciplined way. The unit of work shifts from projects to MMPs. Projects are broken down into the smaller MMPs, and the MMPs are prioritized by product managers or product owners. By contrast, in organizations that have transitioned to the product approach, all product and nonproject work is initiated at the MMP level. Teams pull the work as they complete the previous MMP and become available. Further upstream, customer discovery experiments are run to validate or invalidate actual customer wants and needs. With a self-imposed work-in-progress limit of one MMP, each team works on just one active MMP at a time. When a team is done with the current MMP, they pull the next MMP in their queue, work on it, and deliver it. The cycle repeats for each team one MMP at a time and ensures a disciplined implementation of the lean concepts of *pull* and *flow*. We will explore this model in further detail in chapters 5 and 6.

Establish the VMO as a Team of Teams

In chapter 1, we introduced the VMO as a small, cross-functional, cross-hierarchy team that consists of key representatives who work collaboratively across the organization to drive change and ensure value flow to customers. The VMO has its own dedicated director, program manager, executive champion, and other elected representatives who work full-time to support them. In addition, the VMO has select *linking-pin* representatives.

The VMO's linking-pin representatives ensure organizational overlapping between the VMO and agile teams and also between the VMO and an executive action team. By belonging to both their respective group (either an agile team or the executive action team) and representing that group on the VMO, they help with alignment across the organization. For example, a chief information, operating, or executive officer will represent both an executive action team and the VMO. Similarly, a scrum master will represent her team and the VMO, and a release train engineer represents the agile release train and the VMO. These interconnections among the various levels and areas of the organization need to be made carefully, with the goals of enabling the flow of value and facilitating organizational change. A well-known application of this linking-pin model is General Stanley McChrystal's team of teams.[5] See the sidebar for more.

As simple as they may appear, we know that putting these principles into practice is extremely hard. That is because implementing this network model requires both *structural* and *operational* change—

General Stanley McChrystal's Team of Teams

General McChrystal's team of teams was a response to dire military needs when conventional military tactics were failing in the fight against Al Qaeda. McChrystal and his leaders helped reconfigure the organization of the Joint Special Operations Task Force from a command organization to a team of teams. They tapped into the resilience and cohesion of small teams and ensured their agility by keeping them autonomous. They connected those small teams into a larger network of teams and ensured their alignment to create a formidable and resilient fighting force. Essentially, the task force's approach was to do the following:

- Ensure holistic understanding of the goal through regular leadership communications
- Ensure empowered execution by giving teams the authority to act on their own in alignment with the mission
- As the most critical element, ensure shared consciousness and alignment via daily meetings with everyone in the hierarchy attending

---

that is, we need changes to our organizational structure and changes in the ways we operate. That said, once we realize that the alternative may be to go out of business over the long term, or even perhaps the short term, we can develop the fortitude necessary to enable these changes.

Fund Experience-Aligned Teams by Value Stream

Rather than making funding decisions at the beginning of a project and locking them in for the duration in industrial-age style, we want to ensure that our teams are funded in a way that drives business agility. If we borrow from the venture capital model, this means that our organizations will need to establish a funding model where we can take calculated risks and invest in strong entrepreneurial teams. The venture capital model also explicitly acknowledges the inherent risk in all our investments. The venture capital world is governed by the *power law*, which holds that only a small number of investments will generate the majority of financial returns, and the rest will generate little or no returns. This calls for a very different mindset and approach to funding our experience-aligned teams.

In most companies, the budgeting and funding process is driven by plans and a waterfall structure. That is, yearly budgets involve an inordinate amount of up-front planning, estimation, and accounting work. Once budgets are created, funding outlays are typically locked into the annual budget. The target annual budget is thus inextricably tied to long projects and initiatives, locking teams into predetermined efforts that may or may not deliver successful business outcomes. Overshooting the budget is frowned on, driving very conservative funding toward the beginning of the year. Paradoxically, underspending is also frowned on, causing some incredibly wasteful behavior where departments find ways spend their money toward the end of the year to avoid having their budgets cut the following year. This rigid yearly budgeting and funding process generates tremendous amounts of waste, and it is also perhaps the greatest obstacle to business agility.

To fully leverage the investment in our agile teams, and to manifest true business agility, we will need to transition our funding to an entrepreneurial and incremental model. Our VMO will need to do the following:

- work with finance teams to ensure they understand we will need changes to the existing annual budgeting and funding model and to enlist their help in making those changes
- use yearly budgets to fund experience-aligned teams for longer periods of time

- break the waterfall habit of locking funding outlays
  into the yearly budgets. Instead, make adjustments at
  least quarterly to funding outlays based on business
  outcomes
- make regular adjustments to product functionality,
  aggressively funding the MMPs that outperform
  and aggressively terminating the ones that
  underperform

We will explore these new funding techniques in detail in chapter 7.

Summary

Because many organizations are still structured in a way that impedes agile methods, one of the most important steps toward agility is to form experience-aligned teams. Two key responsibilities of the VMO are structuring dynamic networks of experience-aligned teams and creating a customer-centric model for funding and assigning work to them.

This enabling structure of a network of teams organized around specific customer outcomes helps value to flow unimpeded across the entire organization. To organize around the customer with this value stream approach, the organization must first understand the customer experience as customers consume products and services. Then they can create entrepreneurial company-within-a-company units with flexible budgets and roles that will dynamically support the customer experiences.

After the experience-aligned teams are established, work and funding should be allocated to the teams following the dynamic needs of a product model rather than a project model. The VMO will act as a team of teams, which ensures that all teams remain aligned to company goals and outcomes. Quite often such alignment will require establishing an enterprise-level VMO or other connection with a high-level strategy group in the organization.

Try This: Business and IT Team Members Work Together

One of the baby steps you can take to nudge your organization toward setting up an experience-aligned value stream team is to begin having your business and IT team members work together on an MMP from ideation to delivery. If members are near each other, this can be done physically, and they can set up an end-to-end workflow on a physical board. A similar result can be achieved through videoconferencing and tight online communication for distributed team members if the team is not physically collocated. Either way, they can establish a weekly synchronization meeting to ensure that things are flowing smoothly.

For instance, at one of our enterprise clients, a dynamic product manager set off a domino effect when he moved his office from an adjacent building and set it up right next to agile teams that were supporting his business line. His next step was to align and link his business workflow with the workflow of the IT teams supporting his business line. Then he worked with the team every day to ensure that value was flowing without interruption. Thus began a powerful business and IT collaboration and one that quickly led to a true experience-aligned value stream team.

4 ■ Adaptive Planning

Who among us hasn't had, at some point or the other in our careers, the very demoralizing experience of working on or, even worse, managing a large project? Every organization has its share of large zombie projects that, once started, endlessly continue as if the zombie undead. They become an endless financial drain with very little business value return and eventually either crash and burn totally or end up as very expensive boondoggles. At the root of the issue is a rigid, *compliance-to-plan* mindset that causes spectacular failure on large projects. Perhaps to a lesser degree, smaller initiatives also suffer the detrimental effects of the compliance-to-plan mindset and result in customer dissatisfaction, blown schedules, and wasteful spending.

Making the change from a compliance-to-plan mindset with long, rigid delivery cycles to a *compliance-to-value* mindset is a substantial change for most organizations. The typical organization operates on an annualized cadence: annual strategic planning, annual funding, annual delivery of large projects/programs, annual performance reviews, and annual bonuses. Project and product delivery cycles are tied to the annual financial cycle. In our current turbulent era, this is a recipe for waste and organizational dysfunction at best, slow but sure organizational death at worst.

In our consulting work, we have found that the first step toward a compliance-to-value mindset and approach is to move from an annual to a quarterly cycle for funding in addition to product delivery. Many modern finance approaches advocate some form of rolling forecast in place of an annual budgeting process.[1] In these adaptive approaches, the focus is moved from annual budgets to rolling forecasts that look 12 to 18 months ahead. These forecasts inform decision-making to help shape future outcomes and do not try to predict the future. On the product and project side, a majority of our clients institute big room planning on at least a quarterly basis and sometimes even on a monthly basis. Since all agile scaling methods either explicitly call for or implicitly allow a quarterly product planning cycle, we can plan, fund, deliver, and measure in smaller increments rather than getting locked into an annual cycle.

Moving to quarterly planning can help us avoid several detrimental issues, including *large-project lock-in*, *working the system*, and *negative customer outcomes*, as described next.

Large-Project Lock-In

Whether it's a large legacy system conversion or a larger business transformation, large projects seem to invariably turn into undead efforts that suck the life out of everyone as they painfully and tortuously wind their way into massive failures. A Gartner survey found that "the failure rate of large IT projects with budgets exceeding $1 million was found to be almost 50% higher than for projects with budgets below $350,000."[2]

One of the main contributors to this very damaging phenomenon is the fact that, with traditional planning, we unwittingly and unwisely lock ourselves into long yearly cycles. Driven by the traditional industrial-age waterfall sequence, detailed planning must be

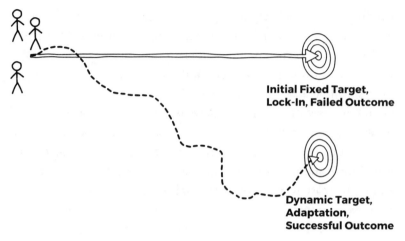

Figure 4.1: *Fixed versus adaptive planning*

completed before we can begin any delivery, and once we begin delivery we are locked into the plan until the end of the long yearly cycle.

Why do we lock ourselves into projects we *know* are failing? Why is it so difficult to make necessary and critical adjustments to the plan midcourse? The rigid approach derives from an industrial-age mindset. Recall the adage "Plan the work, work the plan." If we examine the thinking behind that statement, the implication is that up front planning is paramount ("plan the work"), and once planning is complete, execution in rigid compliance to the plan becomes the key to success ("work the plan"). Any variance from the fixed plan is frowned on and considered to be anathema. Unfortunately, as shown in figure 4.1, this rigid approach locks us into targets that change as business circumstances change and therefore locks us into failing outcomes.

What we need is a more flexible, adaptive approach to planning that allows us to plan for the long term and then also allows us to adapt the plan as business circumstances change. For large projects, that flexibility implies we need a disciplined portfolio management process that accommodates the likely politically unpopular action of terminating the project entirely if it fails to deliver value. Consider how much money we would save and how much grief we would avoid if we were able to terminate large projects before they become undead zombies. It may come as a surprise to some that successful companies do this routinely. In fact, it is one of the major reasons these companies are successful. From Workday to Unilever, they apply the focused agile approach of small batches to deliver on their business outcomes. As Unilever CIO Jane Moran stated in *CIO* magazine, "We've also had a fundamental shift in how we work, from simultaneously running a large portfolio of projects, to focusing on about 30 key strategic technology platforms."[3] These companies don't exhibit the counterproductive behavior of constantly working around the system, as we discuss next.

Working the System

In many organizations, budgets expire at the end of the fiscal year, and budgets and plans are created on the basis of spending from the previous year. We see an odd but common phenomenon in these organizations, especially large bureaucratic ones, where everyone finds ways to work around the constraints created by rigid budgeting and planning processes. Toward the end of the year, managers scramble to find ways to spend their allocated funds for fear of losing them in the next year's budget.[4] This use-it-or-lose-it exercise leads to spending sprees that are shockingly wasteful and certainly ill advised in any organization aspiring to be agile. Well-meaning people end up working against the system. Though they try desperately to work in the organization's interests, they have to struggle against the counterproductive constraints their outdated systems and processes place on them. What drives this noble behavior even in the presence of an ignoble system? It turns out that people are immensely creative, and we will find a way to work the system to attain specific goals. Wouldn't it be a much better idea to align the system itself with the organization's interests and our customers' desired outcomes? A better system would properly channel the passion and energy of our employees and teams instead of stifling them. Employees are not the only ones affected—it turns out that long planning and the resulting long delivery cycles are disastrous for customer outcomes as well.

Negative Customer Outcomes

The most detrimental result of long and rigid budgeting and planning cycles is their negative impact on customer outcomes. Our customers are forced to wait for months or even years for delivery on their requests. When we do deliver, what they end up getting is far removed from what they requested. While our customers' needs have changed over time, we have locked ourselves into delivering what they asked for in the past, instead of finding a way to adapt to what they need in the present and in the future. These problems are further compounded when we have to deal with multiple interfaces and dependencies on systems and processes both inside and outside our organizations.

In fact, within IT, we have a dismal record of failing to meet customer outcomes. In their *Harvard Business Review* paper "Why Your IT Project May Be Riskier Than You Think," the authors Bent Flyvbjerg and Alexander Budzier found that "fully one in six of the projects [they] studied was a black swan, with a cost overrun of 200%, on average, and a schedule overrun of almost 70%."[5] They conclude that an unusually large percentage of IT projects incur massive cost and schedule overruns.

The paradox is that increased up-front planning as prescribed by the traditional industrial-age approach actually increases our risk of failure and decreases our chances of success. So a resulting drop in customer confidence and satisfaction is to be expected. A better process would allow us the flexibility to meet customer *outcomes*, even as we progressively elaborate our plans and change the *outputs* delivered to customers over time.

Conform to Value Rather Than Comply to Plan

Successful modern organizations are able to sense changes in the market faster, respond to changes faster, and measure business results faster. To emulate them, we need to move to much tighter cadences of funding, planning, delivery, and measurement that allow for rapid feedback and fast pivots as business conditions evolve. The first step to transitioning to a more adaptive planning approach is to change our mindset from compliance to plan to what Agile Manifesto signatory Jim Highsmith termed "conformance to value." As Jim posits, "Conformance to value recognizes the critical nature of the business outcome of a project. If we produce a product that's on schedule, on budget, and meets specifications but doesn't sell in the market, we have not been successful."[6]

We can carry forward the traditional disciplines of cost and schedule management without much modification. However, instead of locking in detailed scope for the duration of the project or release, we need to articulate our vision in terms of high-level scope. Then we progressively define detailed scope in the shape of minimally marketable products (MMPs), and conform to value by allowing our product owners to adjust these as customer needs change over time. We will explore these concepts in detail in chapters 5 and 6.

Some key concepts in this new mindset are the following:

- plan, deliver, and measure small batches
- measure business outcomes not stage outputs
- sense and respond to business conditions

Plan, Deliver, and Measure in Small Batches

Making a mindset shift from large-batch thinking to small-batch thinking is fundamental when transitioning from a traditional planning approach to an agile one. Small batches go through our systems faster and with less variability. In a traditional product development environment, as we develop a product, we have large batches of requirements, designs, untested code, tested code, and finally, a large-batch release into production. These large batches inordinately delay the delivery of any value to our customers. As illustrated in figure 4.2, our new approach is to chunk up the large batches and get them to flow through the system as quickly

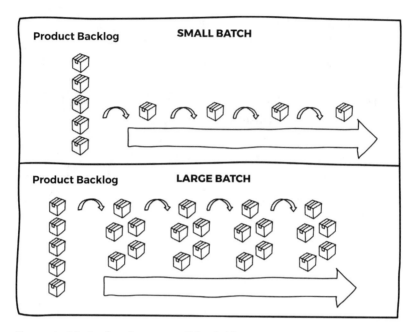

Figure 4.2: *Moving from large- to small-batch delivery*

as possible. In an agile organization, our planning shifts to having our product owners list and prioritize all the things we need (such as features, defects, risks, nonfunctional items) on a product backlog and then moving the highest-priority chunks through the system and measuring progress at every step.

Larger releases are broken down into product increments, increments into MMPs, MMPs into epics, epics into features, and features into user stories and, within a Sprint, stories into tasks, as illustrated in figure 4.3.

We then implement the user stories in timeboxed Sprints of typically two weeks, delivering a mini product increment at the end of every Sprint. Over time, these mini increments are aggregated into releases, and those releases are deployed to end users when the product owner deems them acceptable for deployment into production for use by customers. To achieve fast and continuous feedback, we enable DevOps telemetry. That is, following a telemetric approach, DevOps tools allow us to record and transmit key data from our

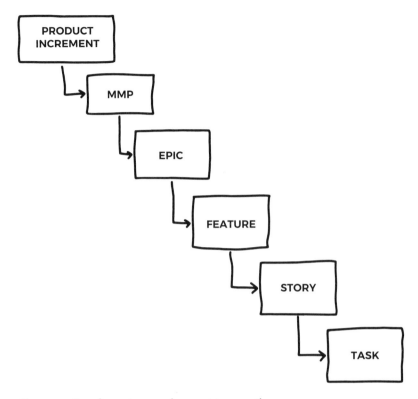

Figure 4.3: *Sample requirements decomposition on agile teams*

products and environments that facilitates real-time feedback and monitoring. That data is then used to resolve impediments and also as feedback to adapt our plans.

Measure Business Outcomes, Not Stage Outputs

Several decades ago, in our personal experience, programmer productivity used to be measured by a lines-of-code output metric. That is, the more lines of code a programmer produced, the more productive she was gauged to be. Likewise, with testers, the number of defects identified was the measure of tester effectiveness. The more defects a tester found, the more productive she was gauged to be. In both cases, there are underlying issues. Since they were measured

Figure 4.4: *Outcome metrics*

by the output they produced, programmers simply produced more code, rather than optimized code. The copy-and-paste function came in handy to easily generate more useless code. Testers, for their part, identified defects, but were not interested in having the root causes of those defects fixed. The more defects they continued to find, the more they were recognized and deemed productive. Both of these are classic examples of *suboptimization* driven by a system that was measuring *outputs* at each stage, instead of finding a way to *optimize the whole system* by measuring value as defined by *outcomes*. The output metrics indicate what we produced (e.g., number of lines of code or number of defects found), without giving us any indication of the business value we delivered in terms of business or customer outcome metrics. An example of outcome metrics that can be used at any level in the organization—team, program, or enterprise—is illustrated in figure 4.4.

Three very powerful outcome metrics are *time to market, cost,* and *business customer satisfaction.* These metrics can be combined with other output metrics like team velocity and burndown charts. Outcome metrics, not output metrics, provide the clearest picture of the business value delivered.

Sense and Respond to Business Conditions

In an effort to control change, traditional approaches prescribe corrective action to ensure that products and project performance adhere or conform to product requirements and project plans. The downfall of this approach is that when change occurs we are required to conform to outdated and irrelevant artifacts. When we do this, we lose the opportunity to deliver true business value to our customers and end up delivering out-of-date documents with little or no value instead. The underlying assumption here is that change is essentially a dangerous thing because of its potential ramifications on scope, cost, and schedule. Certainly, uncontrolled and mindless change will drive projects and products to disaster. But in our dynamic and turbulent environments, adapting to change is a critical necessity. In these environments, change is simultaneously dangerous and beneficial. The danger arises from fighting or ignoring change or attempting to control it. Embracing change with a disciplined test, learn, and adapt approach similar to scientific experimentation is the best way to conform to value.

Being open to mindful change that is driven by business value has been part of the agile movement from its inception. Kent Beck, Ron Jeffries, and Chet Hendrickson advanced the extreme programming mantra of embrace change, and many extreme programming practices are designed from the ground up to accommodate late-breaking changes. A decade ago, Jim Highsmith presciently wrote, "Every iteration we want to ask, 'Does the product have enough capability to release today?' We want to focus on this strategic value question, not on whether every detailed requirement (scope) has been implemented."[7]

Jeff Sutherland and Ken Schwaber designed Scrum's product owner role on the basis of the observe, orient, decide, act (OODA) loop, with the assumption of the need to learn rapidly in an uncertain world.[8] In fact, the OODA loop, illustrated in figure 4.5, has an iterative learning discipline that is embedded in all agile methods from the earlier team-based ones to newer scaling methods. Military strategist and U.S. Air Force Colonel John Boyd developed the OODA loop as a practical way for fighter pilots to apply rational thinking in uncertain and chaotic situations. It has been applied widely in many industries as a means to move forward with speed, intelligently applying empiricism under conditions of extreme uncertainty.

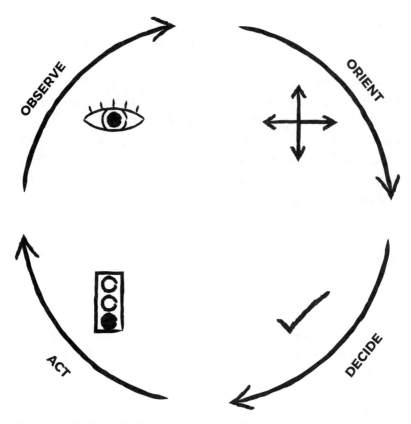

Figure 4.5: *John Boyd's OODA loop learning discipline*

Building a sense-and-respond learning discipline with the OODA loop is a great way to extend the agile ethos across organizations from end to end. Embedding the OODA learning discipline into our planning processes allows us to take an empirical approach and sense and respond rapidly to changing business conditions. Planning, delivering, and measuring in small batches allows us to tightly link OODA-style planning to execution, learning, and adaptation. For example, businesses such as Mondelez International and Dell pair observation via social media monitoring with command centers to analyze, orient, decide, and act in real time.[9] Next, we will explore how the VMO can implement the OODA loop's adaptive approach to planning with its embedded learning at all levels in our organizations.

Apply Adaptive Planning at Multiple Levels

Perhaps the best-known quote capturing the agile approach to planning is from President Dwight Eisenhower's 1957 remarks at the National Defense Executive Reserve Conference. He had heard something "long ago in the Army: Plans are worthless, but planning is everything."[10] Eisenhower's paradoxical statement about preparation is easily explained in our agile context. The artifact of the plan is less important than the interactions among people during the planning process and the learning and adaptation that emerges.

The VMO has a strong role to play in how our organizations plan, deliver, and measure work. To institutionalize adaptive planning, the VMO needs to partner with stakeholders across the organization to enable the structured multilevel approach conceptualized by Mike Cohn in his landmark book *Agile Estimating and Planning*[11] and illustrated in figure 4.6. Mike draws on the concept of planning in horizons or levels across the organizational continuum.

Each horizon or level is distinct from the other but is closely interrelated in ways that inform and influence the others. The multiple levels are typically synchronized in a cascading cadence. Strategy, portfolio, and product plans typically operate on a quarterly cadence; release plans operate on a tighter cadence determined by product managers and product owners; iteration or Sprint plans follow the Sprint cadence of one, two, three, or four weeks; and daily planning happens every day in a daily scrum (also known as the daily stand-up) meeting. Plans are synchronized and aligned regularly across the multiple levels in multiple ways by the VMO, including the following:

- continuous strategic alignment of the next set of objectives and key results (OKRs) against the last quarter's performance and the next quarter's goals
- development of quarterly rolling-wave delivery of value and the measurement of interim business results
- regular meetings to measure and review portfolio progress against OKRs
- quarterly big room planning events to broadly communicate and realign the organization for the next set of OKRs

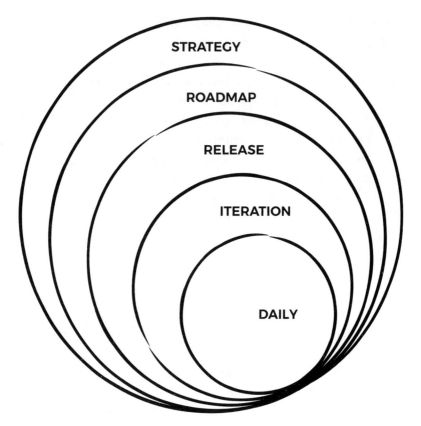

Figure 4.6: *Multilevel agile planning (adapted with permission from Mike Cohn)*

We detail next how the VMO can drive rapid learning, adaptation, and overall business agility using a cadenced, multilevel planning approach.

Conduct Strategy Planning—Scenario Planning, OKRs, and MMPs

In agile organizations, execution is always linked to strategy. To accomplish this, strategy planning is conducted in a graduated manner. We begin with scenario planning, then build out scenarios into OKRs, which then form the basis for product MMPs, as described next.

Visualize the Future as a Dynamic Landscape with Scenario Planning
Scenario planning is a strategic planning approach that is used to make flexible long-term plans. It arose from the military and was pioneered in industry at the Royal Dutch Shell Group. Scenario planning helped Shell anticipate, prepare for, and navigate multiple crises, including the 1973 energy crisis, the collapse of the oil market in 1986, and the subsequent pressure to address social and environmental problems. Instead of predicting or attempting to forecast a single version of the future, scenario planning analyzes and explores a few possible futures or scenarios and delineates the actions to be taken for each of them. This analysis of different possible scenarios improves decision-making by carefully considering each scenario's outcome and implications. It facilitates a dynamic response in the future by ensuring advance preparation for that possible future. A good way to begin with scenario planning is to visualize the future as a dynamic landscape, as illustrated in figure 4.7.

Then to build on this high-level visualization, we need a diverse set of three to four scenarios with different narratives. Each scenario needs context, detail, and multiple strategic options to assess how likely they are to succeed or fail. Typical details might include key assumptions as well as impacts to our programs, finances, and people. A bare-bones scenario planning process is illustrated in figure 4.8.

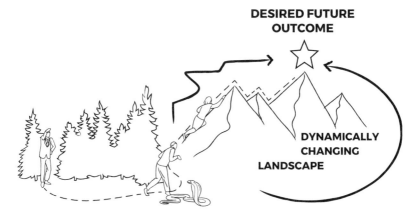

Figure 4.7: *Visualizing the future as a dynamic landscape*

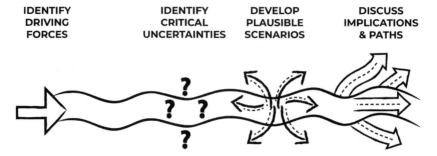

IDENTIFY	IDENTIFY	DEVELOP	DISCUSS
DRIVING	CRITICAL	PLAUSIBLE	IMPLICATIONS
FORCES	UNCERTAINTIES	SCENARIOS	& PATHS

Figure 4.8: *Scenario planning process*

As a simple example of applying this process, we could consider the impact of the pivot that most companies made to working from home in the spring of 2020. At that time, with the impetus being the pandemic, there was massive uncertainty and fear. Not much was known about the transmission of the virus, its health impact on people, how rapidly it would spread, and how badly the economy would be affected. Plausible scenarios included a short, V-shaped economic recovery with a rapid rebound and a much longer L-shaped recession that would take years. It was important to think lucidly about the uncertainties and the various options and to prepare for possible outcomes. In corporate headquarters around the world, executives were surely conducting this critical analysis of different scenarios and their implications.[12] How long is the pandemic likely to continue? Should we retain physical office locations? If yes, for how long? What will be the business and social impacts of a largely remote workforce? What safety processes and personal protective equipment will we need when we reopen? What are the legal implications? Will the current work-from-home trend continue well into the future, and what will be its impact on demand for our products and services? An example analysis is illustrated in table 4.1.

We can conduct similar scenario analyses at multiple levels: at the business strategy level, the portfolio level, the product release level, and at the Sprint level. Obviously, the more strategic the level, the wider the involvement that will be necessary for the effort. Scenario planning at the business strategy level, for example, will require participation from stakeholders from all across the organization, such as in marketing,

Table 4.1. *Sample Scenario Planning for Pandemic Impact*

Business Aspect	Uncertainties and Anticipated Impact	Action Items
Scenario 1: Quick Recovery by 2020 Q2 End **Probability 5 percent** **Business as planned with added preparation and awareness.** **Work from home as an option.**		
Main products and services	• May see drop in new business • Communicate precautions • Signage and policies clearly visible onsite	• Digital product/services development; for a simple experiment, look to future to build out a more complex course

Headquarters presence	• Increased awareness of virus and potential impact on desire to work in the physical space
	• Operational considerations
	  ○ More handwashing, sanitary considerations and reminders
	• Potential additional interest in virtual work
	  ○ Purchase of supplies in advance in case of supply chain disruption
		• Prepare signage for office locations
		• Messaging to employees for health safety
		  ○ Signs, email alerts
		  ○ Illness policy update through legal and posted both on site and shared through digital internal communications

(continued)

Table 4.1. (*continued*)

Business Aspect	Uncertainties and Anticipated Impact	Action Items
Scenario 2: Global Slowdown Extending until the End of 2020 **Probability 25 percent** **Virtual options a necessity, 50–75 percent drop in business, customers not buying new in-person services.**		
Main products and services	• Expect 20–30 percent drop in business • Need to balance out costs	• Accelerate development of digital products and services

Headquarters presence	• Expect in-person presence will drop, and people will choose to work virtually
	   ○ Operational and supply chain considerations
	   ○ Growing load on technology team and infrastructure to switch to virtual
		• Live and virtual options a necessity
		 • FAQs/information page/ policies for employees
		 • Preorder supplies when possible to allow for supply chain disruption

Scenario 3: Global Pandemic and Recession until 2021+ **Probability 70 percent** **All in-person work canceled, and most new customer business put on hold for several months. Total business shift to virtual, plus bottom line significantly impacted in 2020.**		
Main products and services	• Business expected to drop by 50–70 percent • All in-person customer presence will drop dramatically ○ Operational and supply chain considerations	• Begin emergency development of digital products and services • Accelerate business model innovation to pivot core business

Table 4.1. (*continued*)

Business Aspect	Uncertainties and Anticipated Impact	Action Items
	○ Massive load on technology team and infrastructure to switch to virtual	

Headquarters presence	• Shutdown of all in-person presence
	• All staff will work virtually
	  ○ Operational and supply chain considerations
	  ○ Massive load on technology team and infrastructure to switch to virtual
		• Virtual options a necessity
		• FAQs/information page/ policies for employees
		• Preorder supplies as soon as possible to allow for supply chain disruption
		• Invest rapidly in cloud technology and agile methods

sales, operations, and technology. At the more tactical level, scenario planning is useful for preparing for different possible Sprint outcomes.

Drive Customer Value with Objectives and Key Results

First formulated by Andy Grove in the 1980s at Intel and since popularized by the venture capitalist John Doerr, OKRs[13] are a collaborative goal-setting mechanism used to set challenging, ambitious goals with measurable results. OKRs drive us toward progress, create alignment, and encourage cohesion around clear, quantifiable goals. An example of an OKR is:

Objective: Grow Third-Quarter Revenue
Key results:

1. Generate $1 million in new revenue
2. Reduce customer churn from 15 percent to 10 percent
3. Onboard 100 new clients

The *objectives* in OKRs are goals that define what we want to achieve and the *key results* help us clearly measure how we achieve those goals. The key results are meant to be quantifiable steps to help us achieve the objective.

Let's take our global slowdown scenario. Assuming weaker demand for our products and services through conventional channels, driving new sources of revenue becomes critical. However, with millions more working from home, demands for online products and services is surging, opening up new opportunities for innovation and growth. A set of OKRs for this innovation-driven scenario in the global economic slowdown is captured in table 4.2.

As an industry example of how an innovation-driven scenario plays out in practice, consider Airbnb's lightning-fast pivot to their new Online Experiences platform. Faced with an 80 percent drop in revenue, and with devastating impacts on hosts across the world, Airbnb rolled out its Online Experiences platform in April 2020.[14] In just 14 days, the new product line built on the existing in-person Experiences offering and helped hosts develop income at a critical time. Online Experiences allows hosts to continue earning by sharing their passions through virtual Zoom meetings. From meditating with a Buddhist monk to taking a coffee master class, individuals can join hosts in remote locations and participate in meaningful and novel experiences with other virtual travelers. Airbnb's pivot is a great example of how a focused goal with clear outcomes can drive the rapid development and delivery of value. As CEO Brian Chesky put it, "They need to be focused on doing new things that people love. . . . That's what needs to happen to create value."

Deliver Value Incrementally with MMPs

As we saw in previous chapters, we can dramatically improve time to value by chunking our product releases into MMPs. MMPs enable small-batch delivery, get value to flow through our system as quickly as possible, and enable rapid learning. MMPs also allow us to test our assumptions about our markets and customers and to learn directly from them.

Table 4.2. *Sample OKRs for Global Economic Slowdown Scenario*

Objective	Key Results
Determine emerging customer needs in the pandemic	1. Conduct 25 interviews at key regional customer accounts 2. Design and implement survey of 100 worldwide customers 3. Analyze feature usage in key products and services to track declines
Innovate rapidly with experimental product prototype	1. Develop fully functional product prototype in a month 2. Support 100,000 simulated visits to new product site 3. Track feature usage real time via DevOps telemetry
Reduce overhead expenses	1. Terminate or renegotiate leases for all major properties within 60 days 2. Renegotiate vendor contracts to lower vendor expenses by 10 percent
Support growing remote workforce	1. Hire five site reliability engineers to ensure increased online presence is reliable and secure 2. Transition all employees to Microsoft Teams within 90 days 3. Release updated remote worker handbook with current work-from-home tools and procedures

Importantly, the incremental MMP approach allows us to deliver business value early and often. From a business perspective, this has the powerful potential advantage of delivering faster cash flow and greater net present value to our business.[15] As Mark Denne and Jane Huang note in their classic *Software by Numbers*, and as illustrated in figure 4.9, incremental releases vastly outperform a single, big-bang release.

We are able not only to reach product or project self-funding and repayment earlier but also to generate faster cash flow and great net

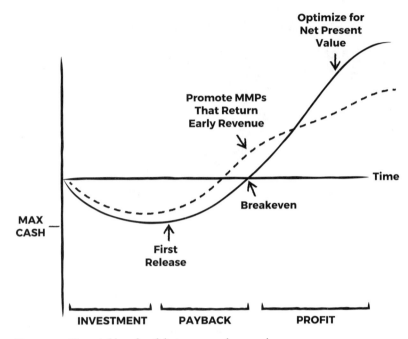

Figure 4.9: *Financial benefits of the incremental approach*

present value by intentionally delivering with MMPs and prioritizing them appropriately. If we need faster cash flow, and are comfortable with lower net present value in the long run, our product owners can promote the features that return early revenues. If we instead want to optimize for greater net present value and are less concerned with lower initial cash flow, product owners can swap in other features that deliver those results. Overall, delivering in small product increments gives us a much higher degree of control, reduced risk, and increases cash flow and value to our business.

Conduct Portfolio Planning—Portfolio Kanban

A proven, time-honored way to visualize MMPs and how they map back to our OKRs is with a *portfolio Kanban*.

Visual management systems, or Kanban boards, are lean artifacts. In Toyota's lean production system, a Kanban board is a big, visible signboard or billboard used for scheduling work, limiting work in progress, maintaining low just-in-time inventory, and enabling continuous improvement. Fundamentally, Kanban boards are designed to help visualize and optimize flow. See Kanban Practices sidebar for more.

Kanban Practices

Like Scrum, Kanban is a popular team-based framework used to implement an agile process. Originating in lean thinking, *kanban* is a Japanese term meaning "visual sign." These practices are deemed essential in a Kanban system:

Visualize the work. At the heart of Kanban is a Kanban board that is used to visualize work and to track its flow. Kanban practitioners carefully lay out their workflow in a sequence and explicitly indicate commitments, delivery, and policies.

Limit work in progress. Each stage of the workflow is assigned explicit work-in-progress limits. These limits guide when to start new items and how to smooth the flow of work.

Manage flow. Teams actively manage the flow of work in a service to minimize lead times and to accelerate delivery. They employ empirical control through transparency, inspection, and adaptation to identify and address bottlenecks and blockers.

Make policies explicit. Teams define explicit policies and ensure they are kept simple, well defined, visible, always applied, and readily changeable.

Implement feedback loops. Feedback loops drive evolutionary change in Kanban.

Improve collaboratively, evolve experimentally. Kanban recommends starting where you are. That is, start with your existing process, and evolve experimentally and continuously from there.

Typically, collocated agile teams will use large, physical display boards as Kanban boards that show all the work being done. In the virtual world, agile life cycle management tools like Planview Leankit, Jira Align, and Microsoft Azure DevOps also allow us to create online displays that make our work transparent. They allow anyone to quickly see all planned work as well as work in progress. We can understand what is coming down the pike, review status of in-flight work, and easily assess what is under control and what is not.

Over the past decade, David Anderson, Dragos Dimitru, Masa Maeda, Jim Benson, and Tonianne DeMaria have brought those lean fundamentals into the agile space with the introduction of the lean Kanban method.

Applied at the portfolio level, Kanban boards help us visualize and drive a continuous end-to-end flow of ideas, prototypes, deliveries, revenues, and customer feedback. A simple portfolio Kanban, as shown in figure 4.10, can help leaders prioritize general demand, shortlist and prioritize demand, and feed a program backlog with prioritized work ready for implementation by multiple teams.

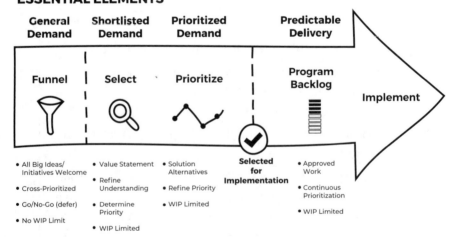

PORTFOLIO KANBAN: ESSENTIAL ELEMENTS

Figure 4.10: *Essential portfolio Kanban elements*

Using a portfolio Kanban is a great way to ensure global rather than local optimization. Teams must work efficiently as they develop products, projects, and programs, and portfolio managers and executives must also manage workstreams for the most value. This involves prioritizing initiatives on the basis of return on investment and the cost of delay while remaining cognizant of constraints and dependencies. A portfolio Kanban brings additional visibility to the initiatives in development, known as work in progress in lean terminology, and organizational constraints.

A VMO can create a line of sight to the organization's business goals as captured in OKRs on a portfolio Kanban board as illustrated in figure 4.11.

Each row is used to orient all work contained therein toward a specific OKR. Business requests, MMPs, and all work in progress are thus linked directly to the specific OKR. Aligning things in this way facilitates a line of sight wherein everyone is able to understand and articulate how their work is part of the organization's goals, strategies, and desired outcomes. It ensures that innovation and experimentation is focused on business outcomes and does not wander off track into wasteful pursuits. It also ensures that the entire team can visualize, track, and manage the flow of value from concept to cash. Finally, it allows leadership to create tight alignment by clearly specifying *what* needs to be achieved and create greater autonomy by delegating the *how* to product owners and teams.

Conduct Product and Release Planning—Product Road Map and Big Room Planning

Once we add visibility and transparency to our portfolio pipeline with a portfolio Kanban, we can begin delivery considerations with a product road map and then align our entire organization through big room planning, as described next.

Time Feature Release with a Product Road Map

A product road map provides the link between strategic objectives and their execution. Product managers and product owners can work

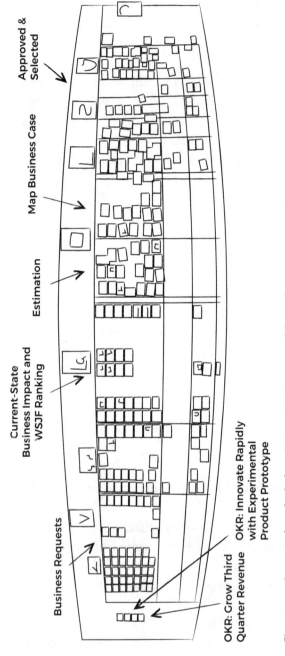

Figure 4.11: *Creating a line of sight from OKRs to MMPs on a portfolio Kanban*

Table 4.3. *Planning Feature-Release Timing with a Product Road Map*

Strategic OKR: Innovate Rapidly with Experimental Product Prototype		
Release 1 Goal: A guided retrospective MMP that tracks improvement and works for remote teams too.	**Release 2 Goal:** Make and share your own retrospectives.	**Release 3 Goal:** Powerful and beautiful improvement visualization and reporting.
Target features: - Moderate retros locally or remotely - Facilitate and track retros - Plan and review actions and their results	Target features: - More built-in retro flows and visualizations - Customizable questions and flow - Tips for moderators	Target features: - Visualize Sprint rating, happiness index, action results, customer satisfaction, and more - Custom metrics - Track and trend multidimensional improvement

with their stakeholders and teams to create and evolve product road maps of desired product functionality laid out over a time horizon. As illustrated in table 4.3, strategic OKRs are mapped to monthly product goals, then to the delivery of target features every month that will help us achieve those goals incrementally.

Importantly, we need to ensure that everyone understands that the product road map cannot remain static. It has to accommodate uncertainty and change, even as business conditions change. Specifically, this means that product owners will have the prerogative to adjust the timing of the delivery of features, remove features, or add new features to accommodate changing business needs while meeting strategic outcomes.

A product road map is expanded into a *product backlog* by a team's product owner. A product backlog is a dynamic, prioritized list of everything that needs to be implemented by the product or project. It contains both functional items like features and defects and nonfunctional items like risks and debt. The product owner prioritizes the product backlog on the basis of business value and customer outcomes and performs ongoing refinement of the items in the product backlog. This refinement consists of interacting with stakeholders to turn higher-level epics into features and then user stories, develop acceptance criteria for those stories, and decide which features go into a release.

Align Cross-Team Releases through Quarterly Big Room Planning

As we saw earlier, any kind of planning is an ongoing exercise in uncertainty, flexibility, and constant communication. This is especially true in large organizations where delivering value to the customer involves multiple teams across disparate functional silos. Big room planning is used to align teams, stakeholders, and leadership on desired business capabilities. It is also a great way to surface uncertainties and dependencies and to reach shared understanding and consensus on achievable outcomes in the near term. A quarterly big room planning event typically involves the following:

- about a month's preparation of team backlogs, estimates, and other advance planning by product owners and their respective teams
- two full days with all product owners, stakeholders, managers, and all team members working together in a tightly structured format
- formal presentations in round-robin style by product owners on each one's team's plans for the next quarter
- intense discussion among everyone on cross-organization impacts
- decomposition of MMPs into constituent epics and those into features

SPRINT

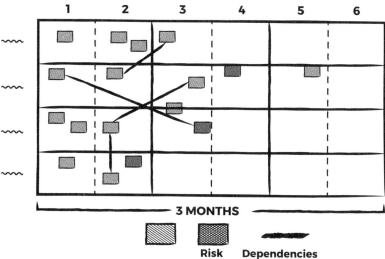

Figure 4.12: *Aligning cross-team releases via quarterly big room planning*

- level of effort estimates provided by teams using story points for all features
- creation of a cross-team master plan for the upcoming quarter, typically captured as an increment board, as illustrated in figure 4.12
- discussion of risks and dependencies and creation of mitigation steps

Conduct Sprint/Iteration and Daily Planning

At the tactical level, Sprint/iteration planning and daily planning facilitate the delivery of value and real-time inspection and adaptation by our agile teams, as described next.

Drive Small-Batch Delivery with Sprint/Iteration Planning

A Sprint or iteration planning meeting is a formal meeting lasting a few hours that is held at the beginning of a fixed timebox called a

Sprint or an iteration. Team-based agile methods like Scrum and extreme programming rely on timeboxing to ensure that we operate on only a few things at a time. Scrum refers to the timebox as a Sprint; extreme programming calls it an iteration. We treat the two terms as interchangeable. Kanban explicitly ensures small batches through work-in-progress limits. Originally outlined as 30 days or fewer in Scrum, nowadays Sprints/iterations are typically two-week timeboxes. As we scale up to multiple teams and employ scaled methods, the same small-batch fundamental holds.

The small-batch output of a Sprint/iteration planning meeting is the Sprint/iteration backlog. It consists of all the work to which an agile team commits for the Sprint/iteration. The primary input to a Sprint/iteration backlog is the product backlog. The team's product owner identifies the highest-priority items on the product backlog, and the team assumes the responsibility of delivering as many of those items that match the capacity of the team. This process factors in prioritization by the product owners, estimation by the team, and intense discussion and planning in the Sprint planning meeting.

Enable Real-Time Inspection and Adaptation with Daily Planning

A daily scrum or daily standup meeting is a 15-minute, timeboxed planning meeting for an agile team to quickly reflect on the previous day's progress toward its Sprint/iteration goal, plan out the team's work for next day, and identify any impediments or blockers to the flow of value. "The 2020 Scrum Guide"[16] calls for the structure of the meeting to be set by the development team. It can be conducted in different ways if it focuses on progress toward the Sprint goal. Some development teams will use questions; some will be more discussion based. Here is an example of what might be used:

- What did I do yesterday that helped the development team meet the Sprint goal?
- What will I do today to help the development team meet the Sprint goal?
- Do I see any impediment that prevents me or the development team from meeting the Sprint goal?

Daily scrums improve communications, eliminate other meetings, identify impediments to development for removal, highlight and promote quick decision-making, and improve the development team's level of knowledge. This is a key inspect and adapt meeting.

From the VMO's perspective, the daily scrum is an essential meeting for teams to inspect and adapt at the granular level and not a status meeting per se.

Summary

Industrial-age models drive long yearly planning cycles that cause deleterious effects, including large-project lock-in, working the system, and negative customer outcomes. A conformance-to-value mindset is the first step to adaptive planning and to building a concomitant learning discipline. The VMO will need to lead organizations in the transition to planning, delivering, and measuring in small batches; measuring business outcomes; and sensing and responding to changing business conditions via an OODA loop learning discipline.

To apply adaptive planning at multiple levels, do the following:

- strategy planning through scenario planning, OKRs, and MMPs
- portfolio planning with a portfolio Kanban
- product and release planning with a product road map and product backlog
- Sprint/iteration and daily planning within a timeboxed Sprint/iteration

Try This: Pilot a Portfolio Kanban

The vast majority of agile adoptions begin on the IT side of the organization. As a result, they tend to focus primarily on the delivery aspects of agile and do not have a very mature agile business planning and discovery process. A simple but very powerful way to change this is to lay the foundation for portfolio planning by creating a portfolio Kanban either in a digital or physical format, as illustrated in figure 4.11. Target a pilot program and work with their product managers, product owners, and agile teams to formally capture their portfolio funnel. Making all the in-flight initiatives visible is always eye-opening. Once all this work in progress is made visible, urge product managers to terminate non-value-adding initiatives and to decompose larger products into smaller MMPs.

5 ■ Tracking and Monitoring Program Flow

Historically, projects and programs have been tracked and monitored along the triple constraints: scope, schedule, and cost. Using these as sole measures of progress has proven to be quite problematic, as scope is often variable, schedules are usually assessed through unreliable artifact-based milestones, and costs vary in tandem with changing scope and schedule. In fact, even as triple-constraints thinking has dominated the project management space, we have struggled to ensure on-time delivery of product scope within cost and quality constraints. Tracking and monitoring project or program progress in a traditional triple-constraints regime has thus been an enormously challenging and thankless part of project managers', program managers', and PMOs' jobs.

Gradually over the years, and especially with the advent of agile methods, we have learned some lessons the hard way, including the primary epiphany that product scope cannot realistically be locked at the project level. If product scope is locked at a high level, it has counterintuitive and unintended, damaging consequences. Rather than aiding the delivery of desired business outcomes, locking scope causes enormous amounts of waste; including obsolete features, unnecessary complexity, and wasted time and money. It has also dawned on us that tracking document deliverables is a fool's errand, because we are relegated to tracking and monitoring things that do not provide correct insight into the progress of product scope delivery and we have no way of determining our true progress toward business outcomes. For instance, the delivery of requirements documents, design documents, and test plans, while important, provides no clear indication of progress toward the development and delivery of the product, let alone its business outcomes.

Agile pioneers such as Bud Phillips, who was vice president of Decisioning Services at Capital One in the early 2000s, came to this realization early on and forged the way to a flexible outcome-driven approach rather than getting locked into a rigid waterfall iron triangle. In a 2006 interview with our colleague Bob Payne, Bud laid out many of the ingredients of his "secret sauce."[1] Realizing that their business group was both slow and not flexible enough, his colleagues and he decided to begin piloting experimenting with lean and agile. They partnered with their IT colleagues to develop a faster, flexible approach that brought customers in from the very beginning of their solutioning. In doing so, they reoriented the relationship between operations and IT, creating a shared definition of, as Bud puts it, "what's valuable is not functional perfection, but the total outcome." Their approach, which is widely prevalent today, applied some simple but powerful techniques. Realizing that flow is what really matters, customers worked in the same room as their agile teams in interdependent exploration toward a shared business outcome. They changed the relationship from "We've got to have a big, detailed plan to We have good business sense, so let's get started and the future will unfold with a high degree of predictability." As Bud eloquently describes it in his now-classic interview, there was fun, energy, and excitement even as they became 10 times more productive with agile than with waterfall.

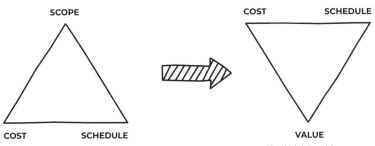

Figure 5.1: *From the iron triangle to the agile triangle*

Bud and his team were so successful because they focused on business outcomes and applied lean fundamentals along with agile practices in their problem-solving. As we saw in chapter 4, sequential waterfall delivery also generates rework and waste by forcing us to work with large batches: large batches of requirements, large batches of design elements, large batches of product to engineer, and then of course, large batches of the final product to test and release. From lean, we know that these large batches cause all sorts of inefficiencies and wastes, including costly handoffs from people in one silo to another, product defects, and the inevitable schedule and cost slippages. Drawing on this lean fundamental, agile methods have institutionalized the concept of incremental product delivery to enable small batches, causing value to flow much faster to the customer, and upending the traditional iron triangle, as illustrated in figure 5.1.

Making this transition to the agile triangle has brought us several benefits. The old model forced us to work in an opaque environment without clear insight into dependencies between different silos, and with very little knowledge of where true bottlenecks might exist. Now we can realize measurable business outcomes as our project and program leaders closely track and monitor the flow of value from idea to delivery, manage dependencies to coordinate this flow of value, and aggressively identify and eliminate impediments to delivery. In chapter 4, we saw that this model enables us to shift our thinking to conform to value instead of complying to plan. Our next mindset shift is from project to product, from large to small batches of work, and to tracking actual product value and outcomes instead of just project document output.

Our old model had its traditional tracking mechanisms similar to Gantt charts on a project schedule. While familiar and visually appealing, these artifacts unfortunately provided inaccurate insight with the illusion of control, based as they were on interim project outputs like document deliverables and not on the final product itself. Compounding the issue is the fact that we as humans are highly visual creatures and it is difficult for us to understand and manage what we cannot see. So in addition to tracking the wrong things, traditional tracking methods did not provide any sort of bird's-eye view to visualize and rapidly understand the big-picture overall status. Now, with our new incremental, value-focused delivery, we also draw on lean to incorporate visual management and visual management systems to rapidly communicate vast amounts of information in standardized ways.

Understand Visual Management Systems

Visual management is a core foundational element of lean thinking (see sidebar), derived from Toyota's lean management system and a popular management technique employed worldwide across industries. It is based on the fundamental concept that we as people process information better visually and that we learn faster from the visual presentation of information than by any other means of information presentation.

What Is Lean Thinking?

Lean thinking is the term popularized decades ago by Jim Womack and Dan Jones in their book of the same name (Simon and Schuster, 1996) and refers to the five core principles behind the Toyota production system:

- Specify value by product
- Identify the value stream for each product
- Make value flow without interruptions
- Let the customer pull value from the producer
- Pursue perfection or continuous improvement

Toyota's system and its supporting lean culture, first set in place at Toyota after World War II, continues to drive Toyota's incredible financial success even today. According to Womack and Jones's Lean Enterprise Institute, lean thinking changes the focus of management from optimizing separate technologies and assets to optimizing the flow of the product through the entire value stream.

In a product delivery or program management context, visual management systems (VMSs) are used to accomplish the management of work by visually communicating the work being done along with desired business outcomes, expectations, standards, performance, and alerts. Fundamentally, because these systems help us make visible and visualize all the work in progress; they eminently enable tracking and monitoring the flow of value. VMSs also help us identify any impediments to flow and can help us resolve them in a collaborative manner. Some fundamentals that are key to the proper application of VMSs are the lean concepts of visualizing flow and limiting work in progress and incorporating the newer concepts of objectives and key results (OKRs) and minimally marketable products (MMPs). These fundamentals are described next.

Visualizing Flow

Flow means moving along steadily and readily in a continuous stream. In a lean or agile context, flow is how our work progresses through our program or product development system. To track the flow of work through our system, we need to visualize our work as it flows through our product development system and organization, beginning with when a customer requests a product feature and ending when we realize business value by having that feature delivered to the customer.

When our system is working well, or has good flow, value tends to move steadily and predictably. When that flow is interrupted—when work starts, stops, or is blocked—waste increases, and the delivery of value to our customers is interrupted and delayed as well. Our agile mindset thus calls for a steady, consistent flow that results in the reliable delivery of value to our customers, teams, and stakeholders. Thus, visualizing and managing our flow is essential to achieving faster and more consistent delivery of value toward business outcomes.

At the Motley Fool, a decidedly unconventional financial advisory firm that prides itself on its quirky culture, visualizing flow begins from their team configuration and workspace.[2] When they redesigned their workspace, flexibility was the driving factor. So now employees can dynamically reconfigure their teams according to emerging needs for the flow of work. They regularly adapt to match the flow of work by adapting their team configurations along with their workspaces by moving their tables and workspaces around. Mobile physical whiteboards and their digital facsimiles make the work and the flow of work visible, even as teams are adapting in real time to align with that flow.

Limiting Work in Progress

Imagine a crowded highway at rush hour in a major city. Traffic is bumper to bumper, and nobody is getting anywhere quickly, as illustrated in figure 5.2.

The highway, however, is being efficiently utilized; almost every square foot of this very expensive resource has a car on it. Given this highly efficient utilization, why are cars not able to move faster? The reason is that utilization and throughput are negatively correlated, as illustrated in figure 5.3.

That is, the higher the shared utilization of a scarce resource, the slower we go. Traffic systems, networking systems, and queuing theory in general predict this behavior. However, we in management

Figure 5.2: *High utilization, low throughput*

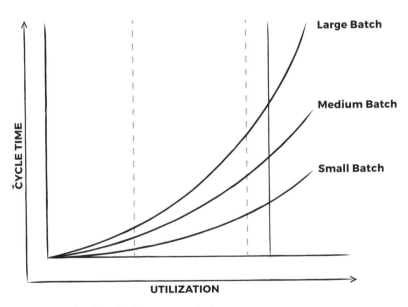

Figure 5.3: *The effect of utilization on cycle time*

have not thought to apply this same thinking to tracking and managing program flow until fairly recently. From queuing theory, Little's law tells us

cycle time = work in progress ÷ average completion rate

To get the work in our systems moving faster, we can either reduce work in progress (represented by the total active work in the system) or increase the average rate at which we complete work. Increasing the rate at which we complete product work is a fairly difficult endeavor. The most straightforward way to reduce the cycle time of work flowing through the system and to increase the throughput of value through the system is to limit work in progress. Limiting work in progress and improving flow in the system is best done by chunking product increments into MMPs.

Improving Flow with MMPs

As we learned in chapter 4, an MMP is a deployable set of minimum product features that address customers' immediate needs, deliver value back to our business, and allow us to test and learn. We can dramatically improve time to value by chunking product releases into MMPs. That is, instead of carrying massive project inventory to deliver product functionality in one big bang, we deliver products in increments of MMPs and improve lead time as a direct result.

Using OKRs to Quantify Value

From chapter 4, we know that OKRs are a collaborative goal-setting mechanism used to set challenging, ambitious goals with measurable results. OKRs drive us toward progress, create alignment, and encourage cohesion around clear, quantifiable goals. OKRs help us quantify value and track its flow through VMSs.

Track and Monitor Program Flow with VMSs

As we've learned thus far, VMSs allow us to see knowledge work flowing through the value stream toward delivery. Blockages and delays in flow become readily apparent when they are made visible. Combined with flow-based metrics, leaders get a real-time sense of where value is flowing, where it is blocked or delayed, and what we as leaders might be able to do about it. The two major elements of program flow tracking and monitoring using a VMS are design and institute the VMS and measure and improve flow. We'll explore these elements in detail next.

Design and Institute VMSs

Our goal with a VMS is to set up a system that enables the steady, consistent delivery of value by allowing everyone to understand the system at a glance, assess the status of value delivery, and identify any issues that are impeding progress toward business outcomes that can be specified using OKRs. From a business perspective, success is judged by whether we meet our business outcomes or not, and any system that gives us insight into progress toward meeting these business outcomes is critical. As such, a VMS provides the link between the people and the data needed to track and monitor the delivery of value toward business outcomes. An effective VMS displays product or program status and performance information, communicates standards and work instructions, and makes problems and issues as transparent as possible. When problems and impediments to the flow of value are visible and transparent to all, immediate corrective action can be taken to ensure the continuous delivery and value and progress toward business outcomes.

To enable easy visual communication and management for a team that is primarily collocated, a VMS typically employs a large wall with standardized visual controls, labels and signs, color coding, and other markings instead of written instructions, as illustrated in figure 5.4.

Practically, designing and instituting a VMS involves these considerations:

- determining a physical location for the VMS and, optionally, an accompanying digital tool
- coordinating with facilities staff to mount and secure the board

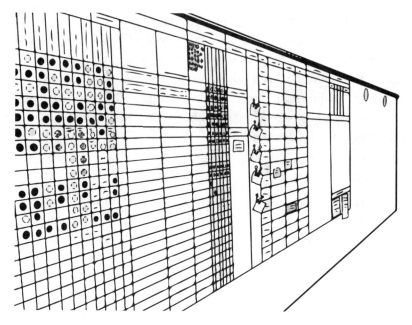

Figure 5.4: *Physical VMS visual design and standardization*

- identifying key roles and responsibilities: a VMS owner, a core team to drive the VMS effort, and an extended team with representation from customers and other stakeholders
- identifying the process, program, or product flow from inception to delivery
- recording OKRs as clear indicators of business outcomes
- creating a guide that describes the VMS key elements
- establishing an operational process that includes regular in-person review, as well a process to capture issues and to ensure their resolution

In addition to the physical representation of the VMS on a wall, we can capture its facsimile in digital tools like Planview Leankit, Jira, or Azure DevOps, as shown in figure 5.5. When our teams are primarily distributed, it is common to operate exclusively with the digital VMS.

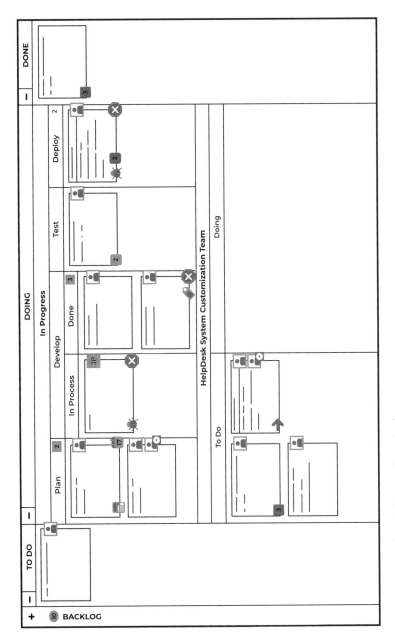

Figure 5.5: *Digital VMS design and standardization*

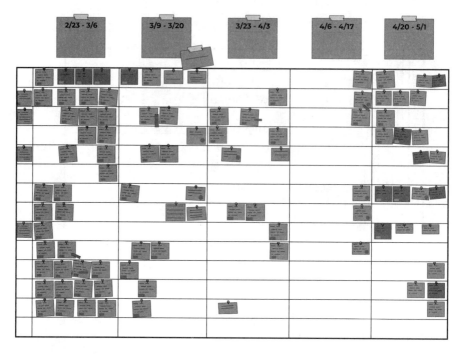

Figure 5.6: *Program-level VMS: A simple program alignment wall*

We can deploy VMSs at many levels, including the team and program and portfolio levels within our organizations.

At the team level, we can use a VMS as a team dashboard and capture essential information needed for each team. Items tracked on a team dashboard VMS might include Sprint burndown and velocity, high-priority issues, continuous integration and continuous deployment results, and team assignments.

At the program level, we can accomplish tracking and monitoring across teams by creating a VMS similar to the program alignment wall (PAW). Illustrated in figure 5.6, PAW was introduced by our colleague Bob Payne some years ago and evolved by a client of ours to manage the work across a bimodal agile and waterfall program of 21 teams in total, with 4 agile and 17 waterfall teams. This VMS creates a simple but granular view into delivery by chunking the work of multiple teams into one feature at a time. The feature represents the one piece of business value that needs to flow from the customer; through development, testing, and deployment; and back to the customer as quickly as possible without interruptions. Specifically, the PAW tracks the flow of work through the system by laying it out in a two-dimensional format:

- rows represent swim lanes of functionality
- columns represent Sprints or iterations
- cards represent epics (large chunks of work) and are laid out as an overall release plan
- dot labels on cards capture interteam and interproject dependencies

Note that everything on the PAW is also simultaneously maintained in an agile life cycle management tool like Jira or Microsoft Azure DevOps.

If your tracking needs are more complex, a more current and detailed version of the PAW is illustrated in figure 5.7. This detailed

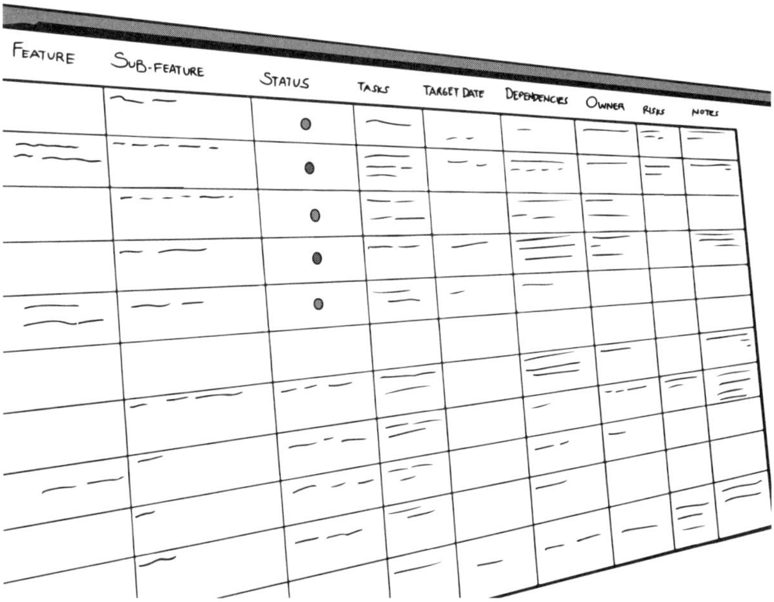

Figure 5.7: *Program-level VMS: A more detailed program alignment wall*

PAW tracks features, subfeatures, and tasks along with target dates, dependencies, owners, risks, and any other relevant notes.

Measure and Improve Flow

By making all work totally visible, a VMS affords us insights into flow and impediments to flow that would not otherwise be possible. In an agile environment, a VMS also enables rapid end-to-end feedback that drives continuous learning. As features flow through the system, we can measure their lead time, or the time it takes to go from initial idea to actualization of value in the customer's hands. As MMPs are delivered to customers, we have the opportunity to get their feedback and measure desired business outcomes as specified in our OKRs.

Flow metrics like lead time are based on the value propositions of MMPs that can be incrementally delivered and evaluated, and thus they provide excellent indicators of progress toward value delivery. So rather than focusing on project outputs as in the triple-constraints world, we can instead establish business outcomes using OKRs and continuously measure the realization of product and business. If MMPs fall short of their business cases, as assessed by frequent and thorough inspections (preferably with real target users), we can retarget or clear them from the portfolio.

Tracking lead time is the most basic VMS flow metric and an excellent place to start. As shown in figure 5.8, lead time is the total time elapsed between the initiation and the completion of an item,

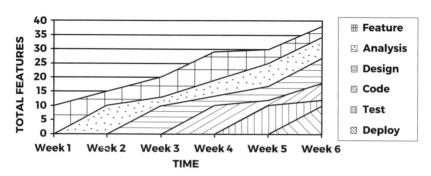

Figure 5.8: *Lead time and cycle time*

while cycle time is the time taken for one cycle of an operation within the total process. In a product development scenario, it is useful to differentiate between end-to-end lead time, MMP lead time, and development cycle time. Development cycle time is the time from putting a story in development to having a story ready for deployment. MMP lead time is the time from when the MMP is created to when the MMP is delivered to end users in production. End-to-end lead time is the total time from when an initial product or service idea is created to when it is delivered to customers. In this example, development cycle time is simply the time it takes to deliver a user story within the larger MMP.

The next task is to identify what types of items we should track and measure on our VMS to apply the lead time metric. In his Flow Framework, Mik Kersten recommends tracking features, defects, risks, and debts as MECE (mutually exclusive but comprehensively exhaustive) items.[3] Tracking and measuring the lead times of features, defects, risks, and debts yields a multidimensional picture beyond that of just product features and therefore provides a more comprehensive picture of overall progress toward business outcomes.

In addition to measuring lead time, visualizing and measuring flow using a cumulative flow diagram (CFD) is a great next step. A CFD can help us identify and resolve bottlenecks to flow. A CFD is an area chart that depicts time on the x axis and the quantity of work in each step of a workflow on the y axis. It captures arrivals, time in process, quantity in process, and completion time.

CFDs help us visualize how work in our system builds up in queues along our process stages over time. We can build a CFD with different bands showing work queued up in various columns of our VMS. Each band represents a column, clearly showing how much work is queued up at each stage of the process, as illustrated in figure 5.9.

Figure 5.10 shows a CFD that illustrates the differences between a system that has bottlenecks that impede flow and prolong lead times and one with smooth flow and fast delivery.

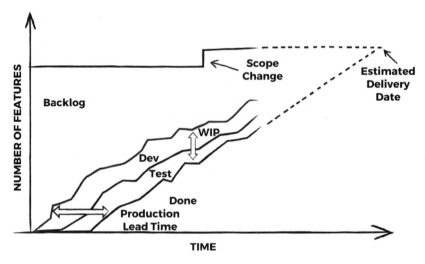

Figure 5.9: *Cumulative flow diagram*

Drive Continuous Learning and Adaptation

What is the higher purpose behind tracking and monitoring program flow? Agility, or creating and responding to change, requires us to continuously learn and adapt, even as we navigate our turbulent business environments.

Implementing the tracking and monitoring techniques discussed in the preceding allow us to drive toward a higher goal: business agility. With VMSs as organizational sensors and knowledge-creation and decision-making instruments, we can track and manage program flow to continually learn and adapt and drive business agility.

Summary

Transitioning from the iron triangle to an agile triangle enables a mindset shift from project to product, from large to small batches of work, and to tracking actual product value and outcomes. VMSs allow us to see knowledge work flowing through the value stream toward delivery. Blockages and delays in flow become readily apparent when they are made visible.

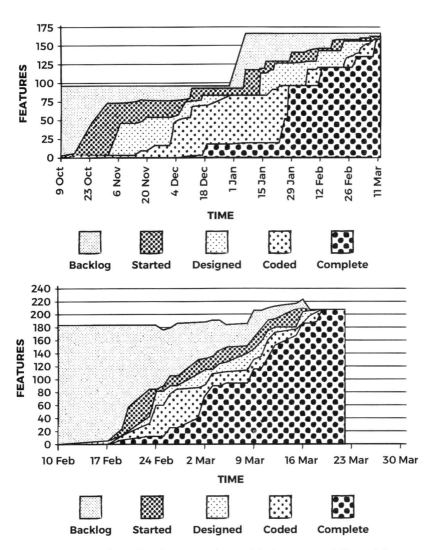

Figure 5.10: *Cumulative flow diagrams with ragged (top) versus smooth (bottom) flow*

VMOs can deploy VMSs at multiple levels, including the team and program levels, to track and monitor program flow. Flow-based metrics like the lead time for features, defects, risks, and debts provide a real-time sense of where value is flowing and where it is blocked or delayed.

VMOs can also drive continuous learning and adaptation for business agility by tracking and monitoring program flow using lean and agile techniques like VMSs rather than industrial-age tools.

Try This: Measure Development and MMP Lead Time as a Percentage of Total

It might come as a revelation to some that as much as we obsess about efficiencies in product development and delivery, the major obstacles to business agility lie elsewhere. Most commonly, they exist up the value stream on the business side or downstream in deployment.

To identify where your true bottlenecks exist up and down your value stream, first measure development lead time as a percentage of total end-to-end lead time, then measure MMP lead time. We guarantee you will be in for a surprise.

---

6 ■ Prioritizing and Selecting MMPs

The old adage goes "When eating an elephant, take one bite at a time." The metaphorical message here is that when something is large and daunting, we need to shift our thinking from trying to get it done all at once to breaking it down into smaller pieces and organizing our entire workflow to deliver those pieces as quickly and efficiently as possible.

Conversely, many organizations take an all-or-nothing approach to feature and capability launch. We try to launch an entire project's worth of features in a single release. Then, due to the inevitable delays that result from trying to do too much at once, we end up releasing nothing on time. The result is a lot of lost time, a lot of spent money, no new functionality to users, and most importantly, no new value delivery to anyone. One of the key goals of the VMO is to release valuable features to customers early and often and to use those releases to start driving business value back to the organization. This approach accrues business value in multiple forms—

increased revenues, improved customer satisfaction, new accounts, cost savings, and customer retention. Crucially, a VMO needs to move the organization toward planning, delivering, and measuring value in much smaller batches.

The VMO also needs to educate leaders on the immense value of not doing non-value-added work. For instance, on one of our recent engagements, a last-minute request came in for a significant project from a C-level executive. With their previous processes, top-down requests such as this would be implemented unquestioningly and immediately. The organization had been resigned to requests from this particular executive. In the past, those requests had regularly resulted in more work in progress, delays of currently in-flight work, and a crowding out of requests already in the portfolio backlog. However, since the VMO we were supporting had recently instituted a disciplined work-intake process, they subjected the executive request to the new process. First, they broke the project down into small deliverables. They then applied weighted-shortest-job-first prioritization to the smaller deliverables. This decomposition and prioritization revealed that the entire project was a clear economic loser. The team was able to go back to the executive and show that the request had relatively low value and was high in duration and cost and that other more economically favorable work would likely get crowded out if this request was to proceed. Once provided with this objective data, the executive saw the light and agreed to cancel the request, saving thousands of hours of work.

The fundamental concept here is to break large project efforts down into small groupings—MMPs, or minimally marketable products—prioritize those MMPs by business value, release them early and often, and then continuously learn from those MMP releases to improve both what we deliver and how we deliver it.

This approach is actually quite intuitive and desirable to many business leaders who understand their markets and customers at a very deep level. In particular, those in the financial services sector rapidly adopt and apply this concept because of the clear financial parallels of investing early and often. Many often evolve this concept quickly to their own needs. For instance, at a midsize bank with whom we worked to implement MMPs, the senior vice president on the business side led his business unit to decompose MMPs into features and then to monetize those features. That is, they assigned estimated financial returns at the feature level and then tracked and monitored those for the verification of business value.

A move to planning, prioritizing, delivering, tracking, and measuring MMPs is a fundamental shift, and we will cover these aspects in detail next.

Plan for a Fundamental Shift from Project to MMP Delivery

For value to flow through the organization and into the hands of customers quickly, the unit of value needs to be small and focused. Big, vague, boil-the-ocean projects and releases are far too complex to be well understood, well designed, well developed, and well tested. They tend to result in massive overruns and low quality. As we've indicated earlier, a much more agile approach is to frequently deliver small, tight MMP releases.

MMPs represent marketable, sellable, and deliverable units of value that are impactful enough to be meaningful to customers but are small enough to be quickly delivered and deployed. The VMO can help drive the change away from the old project-centric model of delivering the whole project to the new product-centric mentality of delivering an MMP. The VMO can most effectively do this by changing focus from project delivery to MMP delivery. The VMO should measure the delivery of MMPs. The VMO can then use visual management systems and flow metrics to drive the flow of these MMPs into the hands of customers so that we can derive economic value for ourselves and for our customers faster. To do this, the VMO will need to provide leadership to the organization in the following:

- how to chunk big projects into smaller MMP deliveries
- how to define and identify MMPs within a project or product
- how to align the MMPs with value streams and customer outcomes

- how to best choose MMPs for maximum economic impact on the basis of desired customer outcomes
- how to drive the flow of MMPs through a visual program Kanban system
- how to measure the business impact of MMP delivery on customer outcomes
- how to use what was learned from prior MMP deliveries to adapt both what we deliver and how we deliver it

Clearly Specify What an MMP Means to Your Organization

It is easy to get lost in the details of definitions for related terms such as MMP (minimally marketable product), MVP (minimum viable product), and MMF (minimum marketable feature). These definitions can be very important to the product owner or product manager because they all represent slightly different variations on the theme and are designed to solve different product-related problems. The key thing to remember is that they have a few things in common and that understanding these common elements is most of what the VMO leader needs to know. They are all small, they are focused, and they are useful. They represent small groups of small features that help the user accomplish something specific and useful right now. There are those who will argue these definitions endlessly, but don't get too bogged down in all of that. Mark Schwartz probably said it best when we partnered with him on agile implementation at U.S. Citizenship and Immigration Services, where he was chief information officer. He said, "Work tiny," and that is most of what you need to know.

Formally Change the Unit of Work from Project to MMP

The MMP concept is important because it fundamentally changes the VMO's primary unit of work or focus. Traditionally, our unit of work has been the project. Everything was about the project: the scope, the schedule, the budget, and the milestones. But here is the first big problem with projects: your customers do not care anything about your projects. Projects are internal constructs that are used primarily as an accounting and financial batching mechanism. As such, they have no importance to end users. Another big problem with projects is that by focusing on the completion of the project, we tend to move all of the delivery of value to the end. Focusing on project delivery practically forces us into the mentality of large releases way out in the future when the project is "done." This may be very tidy from a project mindset: one project equals one big release. Meanwhile, we have spent significant amounts of time and money, and our customers have received nothing from us. If we want to be a more customer-centric organization, we need to start to drop the project mentality.

What users care about are product or service features, and they want them now, with high quality. By putting focus on MMPs or small releases of small features, we change the unit of work to something that is of value to end users: value delivery. This is great for our customers in that they get something now instead of later. This has the not-so-trivial side benefit of accelerating business benefits to us! If we deliver small features sooner, we start to recoup the benefits of those features through new revenue, cost savings, account sign-ups, risk reduction, customer retention, or whatever. If that weren't enough, through early and frequent delivery, we get opportunities to learn more about our product and our process and our customers and make the necessary adjustments sooner rather than later.

Figure 6.1 represents how the agile model uses early and frequent delivery to accelerate the feedback loop.

Set Process Expectations and Controls for MMP Creation, Prioritization, and Selection

As members of the VMO leadership, it is not likely that the important task of setting process expectations and controls for MMP creation, prioritization, and selection will fall to us. However, this is a critical function for a product ownership team. Given any set of customer-related goals and internal business goals, there are likely to be many possible solutions, many different ways that we could possibly achieve the desired goals. Ideally, we want to get several options on the table to determine which is the most viable given the cost, risks, and upside. Determining what we build and when we

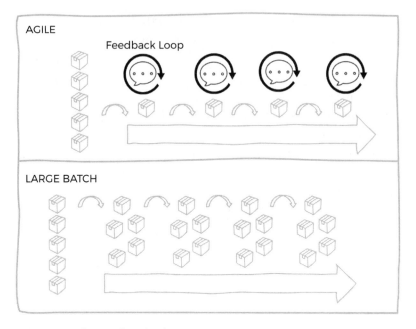

Figure 6.1: *Agile versus large batch*

build it is probably the most important decision an organization makes. If the answer to this question is "We want it all," then we can guarantee that we are spending way too much money and taking way too much time to deliver value. The VMO should be putting strong expectations and perhaps even controls in place that give clear guidance to product owners on how to decompose work and deliver smaller units of value. For example, the VMO could define a set of expectations such as the following:

- Projects must deliver functionality to users at least every quarter, every month, or every two weeks as appropriate for our customer base.
- Releases will deploy useful functionality that creates measurable value to both end users and our organization.
- Product owners will be responsible for ensuring that multiple MMP candidate options/solutions are available for consideration.

- A transparent process will be in place for determining which MMP candidates will be chosen for upcoming release.
- There is agreement on how the business effectiveness of each incremental release will be measured.
- Effectiveness data will be gathered within 30, 60, or 90 days of an MMP release to determine the business effectiveness of the release.

Keep in mind that selecting which features or capabilities that we are going to devote time and money to is a critical set of decisions for the organization. Therefore, it is a critical process for the VMO. We are about to spend significant time and significant money and the results will impact our financial standing and will also have impact to our customers. These are, in a nutshell, important investment decisions, and the process by which we make these decisions should not be taken lightly. Nor should it be done haphazardly and without some level of process rigor. Most organizations put much more process rigor on how we build than on determining what we build. We would argue that what we build and when we build it has a far larger business impact.

Select MMPs for Maximum Financial Impact

Those who have studied lean probably already have a strong bias toward eliminating batches wherever possible so as to create single-piece flow. Believe it or not, we actually do need some batching here in the discovery process. Each MMP candidate is likely to look like a good investment when evaluated individually and without respect to the other competing MMPs. But in portfolio management, we should create multiple investment options and then weight those options against each other to choose the soundest investments. The question is not, "Is this a good stock?" The question is, "What are our alternatives and which is the best investment given our risk profile?" In IT portfolio management, the question is not, "Is this a good project?" Almost every project is going to appear to be a reasonable investment. The question we should be asking is, "Of all the project requests that have been made, which are the best projects in terms of return versus risk versus time?"

The same applies at the MMP level. We should be asking, "What are our MMP options and which ones appear to be the most economically viable?" To make these kinds of comparative decisions, we need to get all of the options out on the table and weigh them against each other in a competitive manner such that only the economic winners move forward. Most organizations evaluate each project or MMP in isolation and simply try to determine whether it's a good investment. This is not the right approach. Requests are going to come in all of the time, and each individual request, be it a project or an MMP, will probably look worthwhile. Dysfunctional organizations will therefore often try to say yes to all of them, one at a time as they come in. The result is a huge portfolio of project works in progress with numerous in-flight efforts all simultaneously competing for the same scarce resources. The result is huge spending, a lot of juggling, and very little delivery. The mistake that most organizations make is in approving all of the requests and then trying to cram them all into an already overburdened organization. As we explored in chapter 5, this is akin to shoving more cars on the highway, as shown in figure 6.2: we get really great utilization of the highway, but everyone is moving at a snail's pace. Nobody is getting anywhere anytime soon!

The right way to handle this is to have a regular cycle of work intake, perhaps monthly or quarterly, where we put all of the new requests out on the table and make them compete against each other. We need to evaluate which ones are the most financially impactful with respect to our available capacity, available funds, and time criticality. This ensures that we don't overload the organization and that we are focusing our limited resources on the highest-value work that can be achieved in the shortest amount of time. This process is commonly illustrated as a sort of portfolio funnel diagram as shown in figure 6.3.

Basically, we want fast return on investment. This helps not only our organization but also our customers, because the focus on speed

Figure 6.2: *The crowded highway*

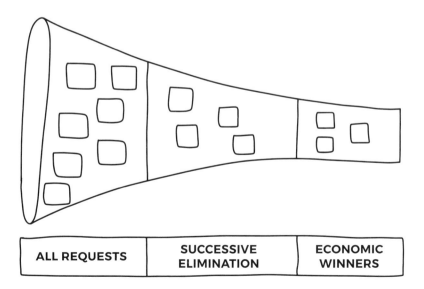

ALL REQUESTS	SUCCESSIVE ELIMINATION	ECONOMIC WINNERS

Figure 6.3: *Portfolio funnel*

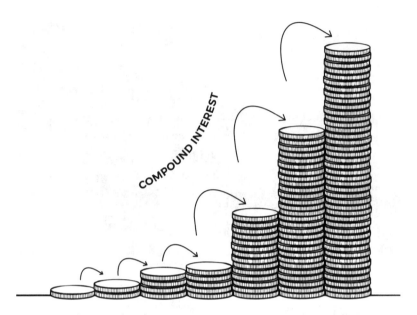

Figure 6.4: *The time value of money*

means that we get solutions that they value to them faster. How will we measure ROI? There are several ways to think about this and many organizations take a somewhat simplistic approach of measuring how much an effort will pay us back divided by how much the effort costs. This is not wrong, but it does ignore a very important part of modern finance: the time value of money as shown in figure 6.4.

Ensure That Time Value of Money Is a Key Consideration

Unfortunately, most organizations do not consider the time value of money when making their project investment decisions, even though it is one of the most fundamental elements of modern finance. The essence of the time value of money is that "A dollar today is worth more than a dollar tomorrow." Dollars that we have today are worth more for at least three reasons:

- Money that we have now can be reinvested into other efforts that further enhance our position.

- Money that we have now is not devalued by future inflation.
- If we get the money now, it is safe. Who knows if we will even get the money we are promised in the future.

Dollars that come in the future are worth less. Inflation will make those dollars less valuable by the time we get the money, and who knows if we will ever even get the money. We also lose out on the opportunity to reinvest those dollars to earn compound interest. This is all elementary finance, and yet most organizations do not put enough emphasis on the payback time for their project investments. If they do look at payback period, it is often in terms of years. Those sorts of time frames may have been appropriate back in the 1900s, but they are not appropriate now, when expectations of speed have never been higher.

Consider the following:

- Big waterfall projects take a long time to complete, usually longer than planned.
- Many of them fail outright due to the high risk of even doing big projects in the first place.
- Even those that do not fail outright often underperform against their business goals.

For these reasons, traditional methods of delivery have very high financial risk. These risks can be mitigated by demanding that investments start to prove themselves sooner. We should choose our investments partly on how quickly they can begin to generate positive returns or at least project payback.

By starting to deliver sooner, we get many positive benefits:

- We start to see if this team of leaders and staff can even deliver.
- We start to test out the product and see if our users are going to accept it and use it.
- We start to test out our delivery process to see if it needs improvement.

- We start to test out the engineering decisions that have been made and our architecture.
- We start to get paid back on our investment.
- We start to satisfy some of our customers now.

All of these can be used to make adjustments so that we start to uncover risk early and start to find ways to mitigate it. There is probably no better way to reduce risk than to demand that investments prove that they can deliver in the near term.

To choose the right investments, we need to compare the time value of money for each request and select those that have the potential to achieve the greatest paybacks in the shortest amount of time. This means estimating how quickly we can deploy functionality, how much it will cost, and what we think the business results will be. Easy, right? All we have to do is estimate.

Expect and Account for Weaknesses in Estimation

Historically, while we may be good at delivering product, almost across the board in all industries, project and product teams are absolutely terrible at budget estimation and time estimation. On top of that, we are even worse at estimating the resulting business value that we think will get from a project or product or release. If ROI is the business return divided by the investment, and we are not good at measuring either, then how can we ever hope to make reasonable investment decisions? To measure the time value of money, we need to not only measure ROI but also estimate how long it will take to see the returns. How can we hope to make reasonable investment decisions if we can't adequately measure what the cost will be, what the return will be, and how long it will take to achieve the outcome?

Most organizations try to put hard estimates in place using actual dollars and calendar time in order to make these decisions. It is not uncommon for our estimates to be hundreds of percent off. Maybe there is a better way; perhaps detailed estimates are not actually necessary. Remember that our goal here is to choose the best investments given all of the requests that have been put in front of us. That means we might only need to compare our options and choose the best; we may not really need the absolute numbers.

Deliver More Value by Delivering Less

In our agile consulting and training practice, we routinely ask our customers to approximate the percentage of software that they produce that is infrequently or never used. The results are shocking and yet sadly consistent. A good 40–70 percent of the software that is produced is never or rarely used. This is a huge source of wasted time and money. **The best and cheapest way to get our organizations to move faster and spend less is to not build the 40–70 percent of stuff that our customers do not use.** By not spending time and money building this software, we can devote more time and more focus on building what they do want. With the time and money that we have saved, we can make that software the best that it can be through intense quality focus and support. It is no trivial task to discover what customers might actually use. They will repeatedly say that they want every feature under the sun, but when it comes to actual usage, the reality is often quite different. Thankfully, there are tools and approaches that help us to uncover what users might actually value.

Use WSJF to Prioritize and Select the Most Impactful Options

Donald Reinertsen popularized the method of weighted shortest job first (WSJF) in his book *Principles of Product Development Flow*,[1] and the method is now widely accepted and practiced. WSJF says that we should compare our investment options against each other and select the highest-performing ones on the basis of two factors: the upside, or what he calls the cost of delay, and the size or cost of the investment. This is a simple way of taking the time value of money into consideration.

Understand the WSJF Formula

The WSJF formula may seem daunting, but it is really quite easy. The formula compares each investment candidate against the other investment candidates along several different factors. All of these factors will go into weighing the investment option, and the investment that ends up weighing the most is the financial winner. It is the financial winner because it generates the most value in the least amount of time. The method uses five key factors to help you decide which investment option will be the most immediately impactful:

- User business value: How does this MMP compare to the others in terms of delivering business value?
- Time criticality: How important is it to have this particular MMP done by a specific time compared to other MMPs? For example, in tax season, having certain functionality in place may be legally required.
- Risk reduction: How does this MMP compare to others in terms of lowering our risk profile?
- Opportunity enablement: How does this MMP compare to others in terms of creating new opportunities or opening new doors for us?
- Job size: How big or complex is this MMP compared to the others that we are evaluating? This is a proxy, or a substitute, for time and cost.

Putting it all together, we get the WSJF formula shown in figure 6.5:

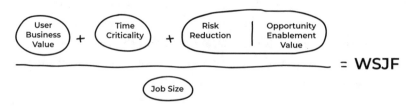

Figure 6.5: *Weighted shortest job first formula*

Ensure That Scoring Is Done as a Group Activity

One of the most important aspects of scoring is that it is a participatory activity that takes in the perspectives of multiple viewpoints. Do not perform WSJF scoring by having one person do the scoring in isolation. It is not a solo activity to be performed by a project manager or product manager. To weigh multiple MMPs against each other, we need multiple perspectives to discuss and agree on the scoring of business value. We need business inputs on value, time criticality, and opportunity enablement. We also need senior technical input on risk and job size of each of the MMPs. Finally, there should also be plenty of transparency into how these decisions are being made. Remember that deciding what we are going to build and in what order is perhaps the most important decision that our organizations make. This is a portfolio management function and the VMO team needs to be involved. It should not be an ad hoc process, nor should it be dominated by rank or title. It should be based on the sound financial judgment of a portfolio investment committee or team that represents multiple viewpoints.

Generate the WSJF Data

How do we actually score our MMPs using this system? Here is the beauty of the whole thing: we may be able to make good economic decisions without having to estimate either time or money. We can make those comparisons by using a simple point system instead of having to guess at real dollars and time. In other words, I don't need to estimate that investment option number one will generate $5 million, take 12 months to achieve, and cost $2 million to complete. All I need to know is that investment option number one will probably generate more money in a shorter time frame than investment option number two. By systematically going through a comparative ranking process, we can arrive at the best investments without ever having to estimate how much they will actually cost or how long they will actually take.

Do not do the scoring horizontally, or by rows. Do not try to do one row at a time and assign all of the values and then go to the next row. The point of this system is that you have to compare each

Figure 6.6: *Comparative estimation*

item to all of the others for each factor. Doing all of the scoring for an MMP at once misses the point of comparing investments against each other to find the best investments.

In figure 6.6, we don't know what the cost-of-delay ball weighs, and we may not need to. We do know that it weighs more than the cost-of-investment ball, and perhaps that is all we need to know to move forward.

What we do is lay out all of our investment candidates and find the one with the lowest user business value and we give that one the minimum score of 1 point. We use the Fibonacci sequence for subsequent numbers and then estimate the other MMPs relative to this lowest one. Perhaps we think that some other option will generate two or three times as much user value as this lowest-value one. If so, then we give that one 2 or 3 points. We continue in that fashion until we have scored all of the MMPs for user business value, and with that we are done weighing the business value scores for all of our MMP candidates.

Now we move to the next column and choose the MMP that is the least time critical and give that one 1 point of time criticality. Perhaps there are other MMPs that have much greater time criticality, and perhaps they have functionality that absolutely must be in place by a certain date. If so, we might give those MMPs many more points, 8, let's say.

The key thing to remember is that to perform the scoring we assign relative points in column-wise fashion. What we mean by that is that we work vertically down the list by comparing each MMP's business value against all of the others and scoring them. Then we go to the next column and compare the time criticalities against each other. Then we go through again and do the risk reduction, and then we go through one last time and compare the job sizes. See figure 6.7.

For example, suppose that we had six investment opportunities. In the typical and traditional world, we might be inclined to start on

Investment Candidate	Business Values	Time Criticality	. . .
MMP 1	2		
MMP 2	5		
MMP 3	1		
MMP 4	8		
MMP 5	2		

Compare All These ↘   Then Compare These ↙

Figure 6.7: *Column-wise comparison*

Table 6.1. *Fully Scored WSJF Table*

Feature	User Business Value	Time Criticality	Risk Reduction / Opportunity Enablement	Job Size
Authentication	3	2	5	3
Authorization	3	3	5	5
User profile management	2	1	1	2
Transaction management	8	13	2	8
Reporting	1	1	3	3
Auditing	2	2	8	1

all of them as they are probably all important. In this model however, we want to avoid putting too many cars on the highway and slowing everything down. Instead, we are going to select one or two to get started with, and we select those that will result in the most upside in the shortest amount of time. We would go through the column-wise comparison and end up with the fully populated table 6.1.

Score the MMPs Using the WSJF Formula
At this point, we have a table that has all of the scores for all of the MMPs or features. We use these numbers by putting them in the WSJF formula to get the scores as shown in table 6.2. As a reminder, the WSJF formula is

$$\text{WSJF} = (\text{business value} + \text{time criticality} + \text{risk reduction or opportunity enablement}) \div \text{job size}$$

We perform this calculation for each MMP row, and the MMP that ends up with the highest WSJF score wins. It wins because, by our own comparisons, it seems to generate the highest combination of business value and risk reduction and opportunity enablement in the least amount of time. The MMPs with the highest scores are our best guess at the economic winners and the ones that we should try

Table 6.2. *Scored WSJF Table with Final Rankings*

Feature	User Business Value	Time Criticality	Risk/ Opportunity	Duration	WSJF	Rank
Authentication	3	2	5	3	3.33	2
Authorization	3	3	5	5	2.20	4
User profile management	2	1	1	2	2.00	5
Transaction management	8	13	2	8	2.88	3
Reporting	1	1	3	3	1.67	6
Auditing	2	2	8	1	12.00	1

to do first if possible. From a time-value-of-money perspective, they generate the most upside in the least amount of time.

Table 6.2 shows an actual example of a completed WSJF scoring table and the resulting ranking. The winning option, "Auditing" in this case, has a WSJF score of 12.00 making it the clear economic winner over the others. "Authentication" is the next-best-performing investment and the lowest-scoring investment is "Reporting."

Recognize That the Highest-Value Request Does Not Always Win
Many of us who have been around the agile community for a while may have been taught to prioritize backlog items according to highest business value and work on the highest value items first. That seems like a commonsense way to prioritize work. However, it lacks the critical element of modern finance, the time value of money, which WSJF does take into account. In the example in table 6.2, the winning MMP has a score of 12.0 even though it only has a user value score of 2, making it one of the lowest business value items in the list. It wins because it has a great risk reduction score of 8 and a very low job size, or duration, of 1. This MMP generates a lot of goodness in a short amount of time, so we should strongly consider doing it first.

Deliver the MMP and Learn

Now that we have decided, as a group and using an open and transparent process, what our best investment is, the VMO should prioritize, or sequence, this MMP for delivery. The MMP should get the attention and focus that it needs to quickly get through the agile delivery process and into production so that we can generate value for our customers and for ourselves. When that happens, we can use the data coming back from customers, sales, help desk, and elsewhere to see how we can improve both what we deliver next and how we deliver it.

Summary

In most organizations, investment decisions either at the project level or even at the individual requirement level are made in isolation. We look at each individual project and try to determine if it is a good investment, and we look at each individual requirement and try to determine if it is a good requirement.

The result is that almost all requests are deemed good, resulting in massive organizational work in progress. Most organizations have way too many projects going on simultaneously and, within a project, are trying to juggle too many simultaneous requirements. The result is massive spending, slow delivery, and low economic value delivery. It also results in a huge percentage of features that are never actually used because they are of low value to end users.

One of the key roles of the VMO is to stop this economic madness. The VMO needs to flow work through the organization toward delivery, and that flow needs to be prioritized on the basis of economic value.

With the VMO, we can manage below the project level by changing the unit of focus from projects to MMPs, and we can require that large efforts decompose their deployments into these smaller shippable MMPs.

Requests either at the project level or even at the MMP, or feature, level need to be weighed against each other. Many requests are economic losers that cost far more than the value that they return.

Use WSJF to find the MMPs that generate the most value in the shortest amount of time, and try to sequence those first if possible. WSJF is an elegant way to quickly and easily determine the relative economic value of requests so that the organization can focus on the work that will drive the most value in the shortest amount of time. This method is solidly based in a key principle of modern finance, the time value of money.

Try This: Limit Product Work in Progress

A simple and quick way to jump-start the MMP approach is to limit your product work in progress to a few MMPs. Give them the focus and attention that they need to get into production quickly so that you can generate value for your customers and for your organization. Once the MMPs have been delivered, use production data to evaluate their performance so that you can improve the prioritization and delivery of future MMPs.

7 ■ Evolving a Funding and Governance Strategy

We have personally had the great privilege and pleasure to work on some large and very impactful traditional waterfall projects in aerospace, defense, higher education, large financial systems, and global logistics. Having assisted numerous companies over the past two decades in their transition to agile methods, we have observed several organizational and behavioral patterns. One of these is an understandable reluctance to change and move on from the past, even if the need to do so is clear and pressing and is officially sanctioned by senior management. As an example, when an organization is making its first moves toward agile methods, we often hear the refrain "But we've had many successes using our waterfall model! We've delivered many projects over the years with very solid outcomes; a few have been great successes." This is likely true for many organizations. They probably wouldn't still be in existence if we had been unable to be financially successful using traditional methods. This, however, is not the whole story.

If we want to dig deeper in the spirit of continuous improvement, the questions that we might ask are, Could we have done better? What percentage of our projects have really paid off? For the projects that were successful, could they have been more successful? Could they have been substantially more successful? Suppose that we spent $10 million on an effort and achieved really good business results. How do we know that we couldn't have achieved a similar business outcome by spending half as much money, by delivering only half of the features (because only a few features ended up getting regularly used), and doing it twice as fast? For projects that were not so successful, could we have found out sooner that we were not on the right track? Could we have then adjusted our priorities and features and approach to better match what the market was telling us? Could we have turned some of those projects around and avoided some big losses?

We'll visit these questions and explore answering them in this chapter.

Budget, Predictability, and Outcomes

Traditional approaches to funding are driven primarily by a rigid annual budgeting process. As we explored in previous chapters, the annual financial planning effort kicks off toward the final quarter of the current fiscal year to prepare for the next. Business unit managers team with counterparts from finance and accounting and work together for several weeks to generate a budget that is often suspiciously similar to what it was the previous year. This plan locks scope, time frame, and budget over the entire year in the hope of creating predictable financial outcomes. The sad truth, however, is that financial outcomes are seldom predictable. The original schedules are rarely met and substantial budget overruns are commonplace.

Common traditional practices include nonagile elements like annualized budgeting and funding, annualized strategy, detailed upfront requirements, and detailed cost estimates. The self-imposed straitjacket from these traditional funding and governance models hinders organizational agility in several ways, limiting flexibility and slowing down reaction time. These are usually implemented in response to a need for budget and schedule predictability. However, given the huge number of budget overruns and schedule slips, it is safe to say that these methods simply do not work very well, regardless of their intention.

The VMO shares a desire to achieve a level of predictability, but the predictability that we seek is centered on outcomes as opposed to outputs. Specifically, the VMO strives to achieve measurable business outcomes within a near-term timebox for a set budget. By operating at this higher level, the VMO can review, approve, and adjust much more rapidly than the highly detailed, overly rigid methods that we have used in the past.

At Nationwide Insurance, the VMO assisted their digital marketing group in the initial shift from a project to a product model. This involved helping set up end-to-end agile teams with business representation and aligning those agile teams to customer experiences as covered in the chapter 1 case study. The VMO advised senior management and helped secure fixed funding for those experience-aligned agile teams as the very first step toward a full product model. While the new structure still served projects, in that agile teams still delivered functionality aggregated to projects, this adaptation to the team and funding model accelerated value delivery and created a much higher degree of predictability around business outcomes.

As in this example, the VMO seeks predictable business outcomes not through rigidity but through flexibility. VMOs need to work with leaders in portfolio management and finance to evolve a new funding and governance model that creates and leverages adaptability as a primary means of achieving desired business outcomes while maintaining strong financial governance. VMOs need to lead the organization in keeping the funding model flexible, as covered next.

Flexible Funding: What Will Consumers Value?

According to the Business Agility Institute's "2019 Business Agility Report,"[1] there are three clear organizational predictors of business agility: flexible funding models, organization of work around value streams, and the drive for relentless improvement. Much has been written about the power of value stream management and creating a culture of continuous improvement. Less has been written about the "how" of moving to more flexible funding, particularly in larger companies with a long history of annual project funding cycles.

While the underlying plans created in annual budgets may be highly precise, the resulting outcomes are often very inaccurate. Worse still, the business outcomes are not achieved at the level that was desired, even if most of the requirements were delivered. Sadly, organizations that use traditional project management tend to focus so much on delivering the project that they measure only scope and schedule and budget and do not really measure business outcomes at all. External focus on the customer needs, market strategy, and competitive forces are often lost, and internal project management becomes more important than anything else.

Three principal flaws in the traditional model together result in a shocking amount of wasted time and money in most companies. The first is in thinking that we can know, a priori, exactly what features the customer will utilize. The second flaw is thinking that we know the economics involved and how much the new functionality is worth to customers in an economic sense. The third serious flaw is that we can accurately determine how long it will take and how much it will cost to build the functionality. Even the most advanced product development organizations on the planet have a long history of significant product failures. Here are but a few:

- Apple Newton
- Apple Lisa
- Apple eMate
- Amazon Fire Phone
- Google Nexus
- Google Plus

- Google Inbox
- Google Picasa
- Microsoft Phone
- Microsoft Zune
- Windows Me
- Microsoft Cortana

The list goes on and on. If the richest, most successful, and most experienced development firms that the world has ever known cannot reliably predict what consumers will value, and what the resulting business benefits will be, then it is beyond ridiculous to think that we, using our long, linear, outdated, waterfall funding model, can reliably do better.

More flexible approaches are the key to creating an environment where we can quickly develop, deploy, learn, and adjust in order to iterate toward a solution that is successful across multiple dimensions. We need to be successful in the eyes of users, successful from an internal spending standpoint, and also successful in terms of achieving business goals. In our experience, we can often achieve the business results for less spend and in less time by simply allowing ourselves the flexibility to change midcourse instead of simply working the plan.

Our VMO can build on waterfall successes to evolve a new funding and governance model by taking the following basic approach:

- Provide fixed funding for value streams.
- Strategize more frequently; annually is not fast enough.
- Monetize at the feature level.
- Devise a fixed-cost model.
- Adopt business outcomes as key governance controls.
- Utilize a lean business case.
- Require frequent delivery and measure incremental business results.
- Recognize that it is fundamentally about the time value of money.

HAIER'S VALUE MANAGEMENT APPROACH

Haier Group is the world's largest appliance manufacturer with more than 76,000 employees. It received the 2018–2019 Global Smart Appliances Brands Top 10 and 2018–2019 Global CE Brands Top 50 awards.

Haier uses **value stream** structures to organize into self-governing micro enterprises. These smaller enterprises have all of the roles that they need to decide, design, and deliver new products and services directly to customers with greater speed and less friction than a traditional-function organization. Using this model, each employee in the value stream is able to get closer to the customer. Each micro business is measured against customer **value delivery.** Each is evaluated from five perspectives: customer value, profit, revenue, cost, and marginal income. Each micro enterprise is also challenged to identify ways to convert customers into lifetime users. This is substantially different from traditional organizations that measure each department against functional targets.

Haier has a clear set of **objectives** that are designed to enable and support the value stream structures. Their objectives include the following:

- Creating zero distance between the micro enterprise and its customers
- Decentralizing to connect every employee and entrepreneurial team with customers
- Flattening the organization and distributing resources throughout the organization rather than consolidating control

By striving for these objectives, the value streams are enabled and empowered to get closer to their customers.

Haier engages in **MMP ideation and flexible funding** to enable the value streams to quickly meet their objectives. For example, they hold "idea tournaments" where employees are formed into groups and try to create and develop high-potential ideas. Higher-level executives serve as judges by asking questions, giving feedback, and evaluating ideas. The format is flexible depending on the organization. The outcomes are small pilot studies and action plans that enable the micro enterprises to quickly begin discovering and delivering value to customers.

Haier's **governance model is outcome focused**; they monitor the business results. They develop metrics such as number converted into customers, number of user transactions, and average transaction value. They also develop nonfinancial metrics, such as interactive users, active users, user interactions, and lifetime users, which help tell the story of how the micro enterprise is doing in delivering long-term value. Instead of an internal cost war or budget war, there's now a "value war" to compete on value provided to users.

The net benefits of this system are the following:

- Decentralizing decision-making within an expected range of performance
- Encouraging the conversion of customers from onetime purchasers to ongoing users
- Motivating new product and service ideas for users. This ensures there will be continuous interactions with customers that drive value both to them and to Haier

Haier is one of the most successful and influential organizations in the world. They have achieved this level of success by making **value management** the core of their management system.

Source: Kip Krumwiede, Lucy Luo, and Raef Lawson, "Haier's Win-Win Value Added Approach," *Strategic Finance*, February 1, 2019, https://sfmagazine.com /post-entry/february-2019-haiers-win-win-value-added-approach/.

Provide Fixed Funding for Value Streams

The lean community has long advocated funding value streams instead of transactional projects. The idea here is that most organizations have long-term stable business processes such as billing, account management, sales, accounting, HR, and more. These functions will always exist, they tend to remain relatively stable, and they will always need support. Therefore, instead of funding a lot of discrete and transactional projects and incurring all of that project overhead, let's instead budget for a stable level of support and dispense with projects.

In this model, we might say that we are willing to spend $25 million across three product lines this year, and we will also spend $5 million on HR, accounting, and similar shared systems. Great; we have just done in a few minutes what most organizations spend September through January doing. We did it by taking a top-down instead of a traditional bottom-up approach, but more on that later. How do we know that we have the right numbers, though? Well, here is the dirty little secret: budgets do not tend to change that much from year to year. In our consulting work over the past two decades we have seen, time and time again, that next year's budget for a particular department or function tends to look remarkably like the budget they had last year, give or take a few percent. In most organizations, we go through months of hoops in order to justify keeping our current staff and in the end, that's more or less where we end up. What a waste.

Instead, if we know that we are willing to budget $25 million toward product development across three product lines, let's set the business outcomes that we are expecting in exchange for this investment. These target business outcomes will become the keys to our governance and controls model and to business agility. Given an agreed-to set of desired business outcomes, we can start to design features, capabilities, and MMPs (minimally marketable products) that will help us achieve the desired business goals. Since we are committing to an outcome instead of to a set of predefined features, we can let those features flex to meet the market needs as they evolve. As part of the governance model, we would expect to see transparent monthly reporting on metrics such as the following:

- functionality delivered
- measured business outcomes with respect to desired business goals
- percentage of budget spent to date
- goals and timing of the next release
- next set of features to be delivered

This model puts clear accountability and freedom in the hands of product management. It also creates a true fixed-budget model. In this model, we don't come back asking for money because we are unable to deliver the required features given the time and money that we have been allocated. We don't do this because we aren't bound to a set of fixed requirements. If we can't deliver a particular requirement due to time or money constraints, then we change the requirement. We break it down, simplify it, or perhaps even discard it because it is too expensive. No cost overruns here. What we get instead is a real and thoughtful analysis of how much a feature costs versus how much it is worth to our business. Product management makes the appropriate trade-offs, and we avoid wasteful process overhead. The first step in this direction is to strategize more frequently.

Strategize More Frequently; Annually Is Not Fast Enough

The model that we propose shifts the primary emphasis away from scope and toward measurable business outcomes. These desired business outcomes come from the VMO. The VMO works with senior leadership and product management to set quarterly strategic goals that align to organizational strategy and then uses those desired goals to approve or prioritize work accordingly. As we covered in chapter 4, the VMO can help conduct scenario planning to set strategic goals and capture them using objectives and key results (OKRs). As another example, assume that one is the following.

> **Objective:** Create highly effective and efficient internal processes that allow us to provide world-class service to our customers. Key results:
>
> 1. Improve financial health by driving down the cost of sales processing by 15 percent
> 2. Improve customer sales feedback scores by 10 percent

The VMO, working closely with product management, can discover, select, and sequence MMPs that we think will achieve this measured objective. This creates a tight alignment between strategy and execution. Using the governance steps outlined earlier, leadership can track the MMPs that have been selected, the deployments, and the interim business results. We can measure whether these decisions and these leaders are on their way to achieving the business outcomes that we have invested in.

Once we have OKRs defined and MMPs charted out, the next level of funding discipline is at the more granular feature level.

Monetize at the Feature Level

To make the trade-off decisions necessary to meet our business objectives at fixed cost, we will need to get much better at understanding the economics of the features that we are building. By this, we mean that we need to understand that some features are both high value and low cost and therefore they are clearly the economic winners. Other features are low value and high cost and are economic losers. To meet our business objectives we need to be able to find the economic losers and do our very best to either not build them at all or find ways to modify them so that they are more economically viable. This is what we mean by monetizing at the feature level.

Customers and some business leaders are frequently of the I-want-it-all mindset. The result is that we have our teams spend huge amounts of time and money building too many features that turn out to be economic losers. By packaging the features that are economic losers with the features that are economic winners into the same project, we lose insight into where the real economic value is. This is not a trivial matter. Given how poor we are at estimating time, cost, and business outcomes, how can we ever hope to be able to understand the economics at the feature level?

The reality is that it is extraordinarily difficult to predict the economic winners and losers and that we will all need to get much more comfortable with the idea of experimentation and fast hypothesis testing. There are, however, fast and relatively simple ways to come up with reasonable approximations.

In particular, the WSJF (weighted shortest job first) technique mentioned previously can help here. With the WSJF estimation completed, we now have a pretty good picture of which features are most likely to be the economic winners and losers. Our product management team should then strongly consider using this information to sequence, or prioritize, the features to maximize economic value. Once we have addressed prioritization, we need to figure out the financial aspect.

What about the Money?

Those of you who know something about the WSJF model know that it does not deal in real dollars and time. It uses standard agile estimation in points that is based on the Fibonacci scale instead to come up with a fast approximation. In our experience, this is quite effective and results in sound decisions much of the time. Business, however, doesn't run on the currency of points. Business runs on currency—dollars, euros, rupees, yuan. How do we get a handle on the actual costs? Some organizations may not be able to justify expenditures or get approvals when the decision is based on this nebulous (but highly efficient and effective) notion of points.

Focus on Economic Value, and Not Just on Costs

Here is a common pattern that we frequently see. A huge amount of time and effort goes into coming up with the precise cost of a project to within some ridiculous percentage of accuracy, but not nearly the same level of effort goes into determining what the project is worth. It is common to see fuzzy and vague or even have nonexistent business upside metrics, hockey stick projections of growth, financial benefits that won't actually materialize for years, sloppy consumer behavior justification, and other dubious economics employed to get funding.

Return on investment (ROI) is simply the business return divided by the cost, as indicated in figure 7.1. We put a ton of effort into coming up with the exact cost but we are comfortable with fuzzy upsides. When we divide a fuzzy return by a precise cost, guess what we get? A fuzzy ROI. The result is that most of our investment decisions are fuzzy. Why put all of the time and effort into coming up

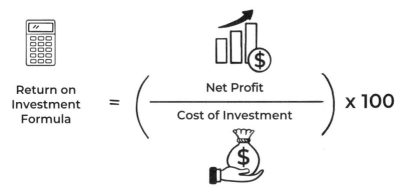

Figure 7.1: *ROI formula*

with precise costs? These delays and activities just slow us down only to end up producing a nebulous business case at best.

Large sums are often spent not because it makes good financial sense but simply because an important stakeholder is demanding some capability. Also, because our financial planning cycle is so long, we justify the lack of rigor in the upside by saying we don't have time or that we know our business and what our customers want. However, we can probably agree that given the huge number of projects that fail to meet their stated objectives, we obviously don't know our customer economics very well at all, at least not to the level that we are able to monetize their behaviors. In our experience, we need to focus much more on the value of the work, why we are doing it, and how we will measure the outcome in real terms. Basically there is way too much focus on the "I" part of the ROI and not nearly enough on the "R." The result is poor investment decisions that utilize enormous sums of money and tie up our limited resources only to result in mediocre levels of business improvement. All that said, in most organizations, someone is probably going to ask to see a cost.

So How Do We Estimate Costs in This Model?

Traditionally, we use bottom-up estimation to come up with a cost estimate. We develop fairly detailed requirements, then estimate what it would take to get the requirements done. Then we set all of this in stone, locking the requirements and the funding and the time estimate. By doing this, we lose all of our flexibility and we often lose a lot of time (and money) coming up with the detailed requirements and the detailed cost estimates. These activities can often take months.

For process improvement folks, note that putting more focus on the up-front budgeting, approval, and funding processes will speed up your end-to-end delivery process. These up-front processes are often as long or even longer than the delivery process.

In the flexible funding model, we don't develop and estimate detailed requirements up front. How can we estimate what the required investment will be if we do not know exactly what we are going to deliver? We estimate from the top down instead of from the bottom up. Basically, we set a budget and our product owners need to stay within that budget.

Top-Down Estimation

In this top-down estimation method, we can work backward from a desired financial goal to develop a business case. Perhaps we have a business goal of reducing costs in some function by $5 million over some time frame.

The next step would be to get a rough budget for this work that would fit within our internal financial ROI hurdle. To justify the investment, perhaps we would be willing to spend up to $3 million to get the $5 million savings. Do we need more info than this? Using top-down financial outcome planning, we would be happy spending $3 million to get $5 million. Using this approach can get a level of investment without having to spend tons of time and money developing and estimating the detailed requirements.

How do we know if we can achieve the outcome with this top-down imposed budget? We might need to do a quick estimation of some of the key high-level requirements. The trick would then be to *not* lock in those requirements but use them as budgetary placeholders. Actual requirements/solutions would evolve as we learn more, and we could update the business case as we learn more.

The requirements and estimates that we come up with are used as a gauge, not as a mandate or a contract. What is contracted is the outcome and the overall budget and the timing. We will let the requirements specifics flex so that we can find the most impactful and economical solutions.

Now, though, we are back to having to estimate high-level requirements for the desired outcome given the budget that has been made available. How can we do that without knowing the details? Estimating requirements in hours is immensely time consuming and often grossly inaccurate. While it does give the illusion of precision, that precision is usually highly inaccurate. This is why our estimates are so often off by 100 percent or more. But there are alternatives that are much faster and easier and that if used conservatively, may be more accurate.

Equipped with a top-down estimate, we can now develop a fixed-cost model for our agile teams.

Devise a Fixed-Cost Model for Your Stable Agile Teams

Agile teams are cross functional and stay together over the medium term. They stay together often for years and so learn how to work together. They become a high-performing unit that has a predictable productivity. The ramifications of this are huge from a cost and time estimation standpoint. Imagine this scenario:

1. A 10-person agile team has a mix of developers, testers, analysts, and perhaps part of a database person and a scrum master.
2. Some folks make more and some make less, but on average, the blended cost per hour is $150.
3. Each Sprint is two weeks long, or 80 working hours.

In this example, the cost of the team, per Sprint, is $10 \times 80 \times \$150 = \$120,000$. There are two important pieces of information here: the cost and time frame. Work is done in two-week chunks, and each two-week chunk costs $120,000, as shown in figure 7.2.

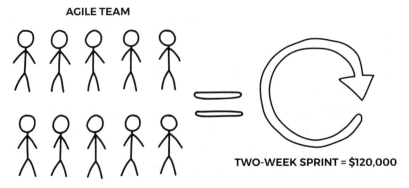

Figure 7.2: *Cost of the team per Sprint*

In estimating work, let's get away from huge spreadsheets with row upon row of people, titles, labor categories, rates, allocation percentages, and all of that. Instead, let's estimate in team Sprints. For example, we might come up with a ballpark estimate that it would take two agile teams and 10 Sprints, plus or minus 2 Sprints, to perform some piece of work.

Cost: 2 teams × 10 Sprints × ($120,000/Sprint) = $2.4 million

Time: 10 Sprints × (2 weeks/Sprint) = 20 weeks

Variance: 2 Sprints, which equates to 4 weeks of time variance and up to $480,000 in cost variance

Wow, that was easy.

Now we have a defined business outcome, a cost, and a time frame and an idea of the uncertainty. This way of estimating is fast and easy. When it is combined with early delivery of functionality, these practices provide us with two huge benefits. The first is that we can quickly see how much of the solution the team was able to accomplish and thereby validate our estimate. The second and much larger benefit is that we can quickly stress test the business assumptions to see if the delivered features are contributing to the expected business outcome. We need to stress test the "R" in the ROI to see if it still makes sense to even do this work at all.

An important financial outcome of this approach to budgeting is that with a set budget in place and a desired business outcome, teams will have to choose solutions that are both impactful and relatively economical. They will be forced to consider best-bang-for-the-buck solutions that make financial sense. This is quite the opposite from the usual approach of doing big up-front budgeting for every requirement that you think you will need. The result is that you usually overspend and probably could have achieved the same business results for less.

Why do we prefer top-down estimation? Because it is significantly faster and easier and, in most cases, will provide the necessary level of control and accurate-enough information. The alternative is to go through a long detailed requirements and estimation activity. Additionally, given that our ability to accurately estimate is bad at best, the outcome is likely to be unsatisfying and inaccurate anyway.

This Way of Working Is Natural and We Do This All the Time

Think of a simple grocery shopping example. We are throwing a party and we need to estimate the food costs to determine our budget. We might factor in certain snacks, drinks, entrees, and desserts, and we would use some specific numbers to help come up with more accurate estimates. For example, we might budget for 10 bottles of wine at $39.99 each. These specifics all add up to an overall budget that we decide we can live with. We get to the store, and we find some wines that are just as good but on sale for less than what we budgeted. We might also find that something else we wanted is out of stock and we have to get something that costs a bit more. We are all totally fine with this approach, and we use it every day to manage our own money. The goal is not to get this exact shopping list; the goal is to have a well-stocked party that is within our budget that results in happy partygoers. It would be ridiculous to rigidly stick to a preconceived shopping list in the face of the new and more accurate information that we gather when we arrive at the store.

We can do the same thing with requirements. We can estimate requirements for budgetary purposes to help us establish an overall cost target, but it may turn out later that another requirement that we didn't anticipate can get us a better outcome for less money and that some requirements we thought we needed might not be necessary at all. So long as we hit our business outcome, we should be good. In fact, we can say that there's a much better chance of actually achieving the outcome using this model, and we can often do it for less money.

How Do We Manage Changing Scope?

A key change in this approach is that the model calls for scope to be defined much more loosely. If a new requirement comes in that helps us to achieve the agreed-to and funded business outcome, then it is fair play. However, if a requirement comes in that does not directly tie to the business outcome, then it will likely not be in scope. If there is an expectation that a requirement will be delivered and it is determined that the requirement is not needed to achieve the outcome, then we will not need to spend time and money delivering it. This sort of thinking can greatly cut time and costs, since most projects have many requirements that are hitching a free ride and do not clearly contribute to measurable business outcomes.

In this model, requirements will evolve and change, and this would be evidence that the process is working! We *should be* changing our requirements as we learn more about how the customer behaves, as we learn more about the economics of this situation, and as we learn more about the outcomes of our technical decisions. If the requirements are not changing, then we are not learning.

Changes in requirements do not break our governance/control model because our model isn't based on requirements: it is based on outcomes. The change management challenge then becomes one of frequent communications and alignment and transparency. Various VMO meetings, customer meetings, backlog prioritizations, release planning meetings, Sprint planning meetings, backlog reports, and other avenues exist for maintaining communications, creating visibility, and managing change so that we can stay aligned. Alignment is around the goal, and we need to be flexible if we are going to use the latest information to help us meet that goal.

If there is no fixed scope, then how do we measure progress? How will we know where we are and when we'll be done? The answer lies in adopting business outcomes as key governance controls.

Adopt Business Outcomes as Key Governance Controls

In this model, commitment is at the business outcome level, not at the requirement level. Figure 7.3 shows the basic governance process. The project is funded to achieve an outcome, so the commitment is at the outcome level. The requirements are then allowed to flex in order to achieve the commitment. The product manager, project manager, architect, and other key parties are now on the hook to discover solutions that are both effective and economical and fast. Business outcomes should be measured at regular intervals to determine if the project is meeting its business goals. Wait! Measure regular business outcomes? That's too late! The project will be over before we can measure against the controls, right? Wrong! Not if you are delivering into production often and are measuring feature usage and business outcomes. *Agile* doesn't mean "development Sprints," it means frequent delivery, getting feedback, and making adjustments based on what the data is telling us.

Bear in mind that we greatly favor a pure value-stream-based flexible funding model such as that described earlier. In that model, we would fund the value stream at a level that is likely to be similar to previous years with adjustments as needed for unusually large efforts or contractions. However, for many organizations, this may be too much change too soon. For those desiring a less disruptive

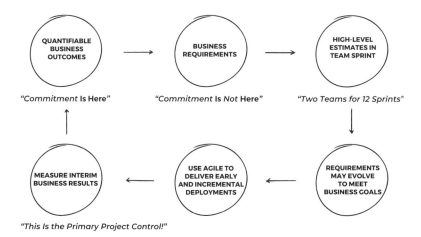

Figure 7.3: *Outcome-based governance model*

approach, we could try an outcome-based funding process. In this model, organizations can continue to fund projects but they would base the project funding on business outcomes instead of detailed scope as the primary form of governance. In this model, we maintain a project-centric model as opposed to a fixed-funding value-stream model.

In this model, the VMO could fund a project for $X million to achieve some desired business outcome such as account growth, cost reduction, compliance with a regulation, or parity with a competitor. In this outcome-based project, we still have a project, but the primary financial governance is around the business case, which comprises the business outcome, the spend, and the time frame but not the requirements scope. For example, we might say that sales order processing needs all the following:

- costs reduced by 15 percent
- cost reduction achieved by the end of year
- costs remain within a budget of $4 million
- processing funded incrementally on the basis of quarterly demonstration of results

Organizations do not have to abandon projects entirely to achieve business agility. They can still have projects with a defined and measurable business-outcome target, a time frame, and a budgeted dollar amount, allowing the requirements to flex to meet the business needs and customer needs. This gives the flexibility to add, change, and remove requirements as needed to achieve the outcome. In this model, the business outcome is what counts, but we do still have some of the old project parameters in place:

- We still have a budget.
- We still have a time frame.
- We have a means of control (frequent demonstration of business results).
- What we do *not* have is fixed scope.

Using this funding model, combined with early delivery of functionality and an experimental mindset, we should start to see early and measurable financial results, cost savings, revenues, new users, lower dropout rates, and more. If we don't, we can learn from the results and quickly pivot to functionality and features that will provide the results that we are looking for. These actual results can be measured against the monies spent to date to see if the ROI financials are still making sense.

This sort of approach could be the basis for an interim funding model that will allow us to maintain projects for a while longer while we begin to get adept at outcome-based funding and governance. Hopefully, over time, we will begin to realize that we might not even need projects at all anymore.

Utilize a Lean Business Case

One way to help drive business agility is to utilize a lean approach to business cases. In many organizations, business cases are far too detailed, and that level of detail removes our ability to flex and pivot as needed. By capturing requirements at too low a level, we end up painting ourselves into a corner. The detailed requirements then end up becoming the driver of success instead of the business results becoming the driver. However, we probably do still need some sort of a business case to justify and document our investment. A lean business case can provide the answer. A lean business case will be at a higher level of abstraction. It will focus on the business goals, desired timeframes, major functionality or capabilities to be delivered, and high-level estimates. Given that it is not unusual for estimates of time and money to end up being hundreds of percent off using our traditional approaches, it is relatively safe to say that we can live without the details if for no other reason than the details are often wrong anyway. A lightweight business case, seen in figure 7.4, would be a smaller artifact of only a few pages that would likely have the following elements:

- The business problem to be solved
- The importance, severity, or magnitude of this business problem

- The new capabilities or high-level features that the solution will provide
- The business outcome that will be achieved and how it will be measured
- The constraints or nonfunctional requirements that we need to address
- A release road map that gives approximate timing for which features will be delivered when
- A requested working budget that the team will stay within

We have helped clients implement such business cases, so we know this can be done. Some lean business cases have been as small as four pages. Such lean business cases not only provide flexibility but also are much faster to produce and review. Managers often spend months preparing highly detailed business cases. Given what leaders make in terms of salary, this is an extraordinary cost in terms of time and money. Lean business cases are smaller, faster, and cheaper and can be just as effective. If this weren't enough, they also provide us with the flexibility that we need to rapidly adapt to the changing needs of our customers.

BUSINESS PROBLEM	PROBLEM SEVERITY/ IMPORTANCE
New Capabilities or High-Level Features That the Solution Will Provide	Business Outcome (& How It Will Be Measured)
Constraints or Nonfunctional Requirements	Requested Working Budget
Approximate Release Road Map (Approximate Timing of When Features Will Be Delivered)	

Figure 7.4. *Lightweight lean business case*

Require Frequent Delivery, and Measure Incremental Business Results

The lean business case focuses primarily on the desired outcome. To measure progress toward the business outcome, the VMO must move the organization toward requiring interim releases to production that allow us to get objective data on the performance of this project. The only measure that matters is actual incremental business results. The flexible funding model we have paid out thus far is based on the achievement of business outcomes. The control, therefore, is predicated on getting real business feedback, measuring performance against the business goals, and adjusting the product requirements to achieve the business outcome. If we don't deliver something, then we don't get the feedback, and we can't make the pivots necessary to be successful.

In exchange for flexible funding, VMO leaders need to work with finance and other leaders to require early and frequent delivery. They also need to demand measurable operational data from agile teams that can be used to assess the business outcome and drive financial performance. Without this, we have nothing more than a waterfall project with a blank check.

Here is where finance and accounting can be drivers of business agility. By demanding early and frequent operational data that can be used to justify continued spending, the business achieves financial results sooner and gets massively more visibility into the viability of projects than it ever did before in its old plan-the-work-and-work-the-plan model.

What about Capital Expenditure? Traditionally, capital expenditure (CapEx) has been managed using waterfall phases with the early phases being expensed, later development and test phases being capitalized, and any work done after deployment being expensed once again. In an agile delivery model, we are performing analysis, design, development, testing, production deployment, and break-fix activities simultaneously. Obviously, a phased approach to capital and expense management will not work here. Luckily, we can manage CapEx using other means. The most obvious, and perhaps even more accurate than the traditional approach, is to use the actual work items or tasks themselves instead of phases.

Using an agile project management tool that tracks stories and tasks, we can say that new feature or functionality story development is capitalized, defect stories are expensed, and testing tasks for new functionality are capitalized. In this way, we can measure the actual amount of work going to expense versus capital.

In some cases, the organization may have capital versus expense targets or ratios that they need to maintain. In these cases, we could work backward and give our product owners "budgets" for capital and for expense. If this were needed, we could say that 40 percent of the backlog items can be expensed but the rest must be capitalizable, for example. In this way, we are engineering a financial outcome by prioritizing our backlog in line with CapEx guidelines.

But things get more complex after we have an initial deployment to production of an MMP or other minimal solution. If we continue to add on to this minimal solution, is it capital or expense? If the add-on work offers new or enhanced functionality then it probably should be capitalized. If new work is maintenance or a defect fix then it should be expensed. But some firms have more rigid internal rules around this, such as "Any work done to support the release after deployment should be expensed" or "A new software version release is synonymous with a project." In these cases, we may need to work with accounting to design smarter and more accurate rules that are still in alignment with generally accepted accounting principles.

In these cases, it can be helpful to put more fine-grained definitions around the word *release*. For example, if we are deploying new code to production every few weeks, is each new deployment a new release? Deployment and release do not necessarily have to be synonymous. A new version or release of software could be delivered through many individual deployments.

The CapEx topic has historically been tricky, but most auditors have by now seen many companies go down the agile path and will have some experience in how to handle these situations. So the CapEx problem is now readily solvable with an agile project management tool of some sort that we can use to tag or categorize stories and tasks so that they can receive the most appropriate accounting treatment. The result should be more accuracy, not less.

Recognize That It Is Fundamentally about the Time Value of Money

It is amazing that even the largest and most sophisticated firms do not often focus sufficiently on the time value of money with respect to project and product work. Everyone should understand that a dollar today is worth more than a dollar next year for a variety of reasons. Yet, remarkably few organizations require their project and product investments to deliver dollars back to the business sooner rather than later.

The financial investment advisory firm the Motley Fool explains it this way: "Time value of money is one of the most basic fundamentals in all of finance. The underlying principle is that a dollar in your hand today is worth more than a dollar you will receive in the future because a dollar in hand today can be invested to turn into more money in the future. Additionally, there is always a risk that a dollar that you are supposed to receive in the future won't actually be paid to you."[2]

A couple of concepts here we should more deeply explore. The first is that a dollar in hand can be invested now, and the second is that dollars you are supposed to receive in the future may not materialize. We typically invest in projects to be paid a return. Projects are usually expected to reduce costs, increase revenues, improve efficiencies, and reduce risks. This means that most of our projects should be paying us back not only for the cost of the project but also for additional gains.

In most organizations, the demand for projects greatly exceeds the funds and capacity available, resulting in many unfunded project requests. Imagine what we could do if all of these investments could start paying us back sooner. We'd have more money to fund more work, and we'd become even more accomplished. The key is to force projects to start to pay us back sooner.

Agile and DevOps techniques give us the tools to accelerate both deployment and payback. By focusing efforts on a few features that we believe are economic winners, and using agile to design, deliver, and deploy those solutions quickly, we can start to reduce costs now. We can start to bring in more revenues now. This generates more money and it generates it now, so that we can start to make those additional investments, just as the Motley Fool said in the preceding quote.

What if we make these deployments and we don't see the uptick in revenue or the downturn in costs? This is where the second part of the time value of money definition comes in. As the Motley Fool's definition stated, "There is always a risk that a dollar that you are supposed to receive in the future won't actually be paid to you." By using early deployments, we can start to see that some of these projects are not going to be able to pay us back. We can see sooner rather than later that the economics just aren't there. The calculated upsides were faulty and our estimated costs were low. Using agile delivery, we can see that we aren't going to get paid back, and we can start considering whether to cancel or redirect these efforts.

An agile and financially disciplined organization would heavily tilt funding toward those projects and products that can achieve positive financial impact sooner rather than later.

Summary

Funding and governance can be serious barriers to or enablers of organizational agility. The VMO can provide strong leadership that moves funding and governance toward key flexible practices that get investments to pay back sooner. To make this work, the VMO will need to educate leaders and to get clearance and support from senior finance sponsors to evolve a new model.

We can focus on metrics for the time value of money to achieve more frequent delivery of value, lower risk, and more frequent measurement of project economics. Working this way would allow us to make smaller bets, which are much lower risk. We make these smaller bets through a flexible funding process.

A flexible funding model along with more frequent strategizing helps to create an environment that lends itself to quick development, deployment, and learning. In this model, we provide fixed funding for value streams. We find economic losers by monetizing at the feature level and by doing our very best to either not build them at all or find ways to modify them so that they are more economically viable.

We use business outcomes as key governance controls, using lightweight lean business cases to document and justify investments, capturing requirements at a high level.

Try This: Pilot Fixed Funding on a Few Value Streams

To evolve a new funding and governance model is a complex undertaking that will understandably take a long time. To jump-start this critical work, and get some quick wins, your VMO should get leadership buy-in to run a few pilot value streams that use the fixed-funding model presented in this chapter. Then you can use those pilot results to incrementally formalize your new budgeting model, working with finance and other internal groups.

8 ■ Managing Organizational Change

In our experience, transformations do not fail because of technology, architecture, governance, processes, or even regulatory concerns. Rather, the two most common causes for transformation failure are the *lack of clear and well-executed long-term change management strategy* and the *lack of constancy of purpose*. It turns out that the soft stuff is the hard stuff. We can overcome these long odds for our agile and digital transformations, but it takes a committed effort over the long term. The VMO is well situated to help drive long-term change and help the entire organization hew to its enduring purpose.

Historically, and in contrast, few traditional project management offices (PMOs) are situated to drive change. In fact, a PMO is typically designed and charged with maintaining the status quo by ensuring that the traditional processes are well documented and followed pedantically. How then does the PMO evolve and become the driver of change and constancy of purpose? This chapter provides future VMO leaders with the tools that they need to become organizational change leaders. To successfully change organizational behavior across the board and over the long haul, leaders will need to do the following:

- have a believable and passionate reason for why change is absolutely essential
- have data and stories that demonstrate that the new approach is relevant to the firm's situation and goals
- have the change be a stated objective in the overall organizational strategy, and have executives be accountable for the initiative's success
- allocate funding to the change initiative
- demonstrate quick wins to gain momentum and definitively prove out the new model
- design and support a long-term training and education model that touches every part of the organization
- create a multilevel, multifunction leadership team that is accountable for driving the change
- leverage early wins and momentum and incrementally add additional projects or teams to the initiative
- design and implement a sustained omnichannel communications effort to market and support the change over a substantial length of time

This set of goals provides the foundation for a change management playbook that will take retrograde PMOs and launch them into new territory where they shine as dynamic VMOs that lead change instead of impeding it.

Recognize That Change Is Extraordinarily Difficult

Behavioral change is extraordinarily difficult. Those of us who have tried to lose weight, quit smoking, or stop drinking know that even changing oneself can sometimes seem impossible. To change the firmly embedded behaviors of hundreds or thousands of people in an organization is one of the greatest challenges in management. Many leaders do not recognize that this will be their most likely stumbling block. There are several reasons for the difficulty. The main one is neurological wiring. Our old ways of working and functioning are firmly embedded within us through our education, upbringing, beliefs, and learned processes; who we were hired by and why, evaluations, and job descriptions; and a host of other contributing factors, even our biochemistry.

As individuals and as an organization, we have acquired deep learning on how to get things done in certain ways, and most of us have been successful working in these ways. In most organizations, when there is a nontrivial task to accomplish, various people start getting it done, often with minimal orchestration. Things just start to happen because the organization has performed this activity many times, and the behaviors and actions are now codified and somewhat automatic. These learnings are embedded in us and in our organizations and they are not going away, perhaps ever.

Understand That Organizations Are Wired, Just as Individuals Are

Some behaviors are encoded in our neurological pathways and they never really go away. Certainly as individuals and as organizations, we can learn new ways of doing things, but our old embedded behaviors will still be there in the subconscious, waiting, and ready to creep back in as soon as we let our guard down. As they say, "Neurons that fire together, wire together." The meaning is that the more we run a behavioral pattern, the more established it becomes. To change behavior, we will need to add new learned pathways through additional training and education and practice to form and institutionalize new circuits of behavior. As we learn new ways to do things, our brains develop new secondary pathways, but the old paths have not been deleted. They are still in there, and in times of stress or confusion or frustration or in a lapse of concentration the old, default pathways will get activated. Multiply this by the hundreds or thousands of people in your organization and it is easy to see why the old ways will keep reappearing over and over again. They're like weeds; we can keep pulling them out, but they just keep slowly growing back unless we can change the default behavior.

Begin with Leadership Alignment

On top of the challenges provided by this natural neural pathway approach to change, there is the added challenge of misalignment. Many of us cling dearly to our beliefs. We certainly see this in the political realm, and we see all of the societal dysfunction to which this can lead. Organizationally, we have leaders and influencers who have strong beliefs about how things should be done, and there will be disagreement among them. This will lead to fractured and inconsistent messages from our leaders, half-hearted or reluctant buy-in, or even antagonism (figure 8.1). These fractures are exactly the chinks in the armor that will get exploited. The mixed signals from leadership will provide ample opportunity for old ways of working to continue to thrive. The result is that the change will happen more slowly than we would like, or it may not happen at all.

The net result of all of this is that organizational change management continues to be one of the most difficult leadership undertakings. Luckily, this fact is relatively well known, and there is a wealth

Figure 8.1: *Misaligned leadership*

of research, tools, and techniques for managing change. The trick is knowing ourselves and our organizations well enough to recognize that we need this help.

Spend More Time on the Soft Stuff

Many of us become leaders through some technical path. We are good at engineering, accounting, project management, writing, law, finance, or some other specific discipline. We therefore tend to find our solutions through the lens of our known disciplines. If we are having technical issues, we look for the answers in architecture or system design. If we are having issues with cost and schedule, we look for answers in estimation and more advanced use of project management tools. However, we are typically not so good at looking beyond our areas of expertise for the answers to our problems. The result is that if we are having agile process problems, we continue to look to yet more agile processes for the answers. We do not tend to look for answers in individual behavioral change, organizational change management, or other "soft stuff."

The most successful agile organizations have one clear advantage over others. The successful ones have leaders who understand organizational change and who have designed and executed a holistic organizational change strategy. We have come to believe that this is a cornerstone of organizations that are successful over the long term. These organizations are able to change and adapt to new business landscapes, new technologies, and changing customer demographics because they have a repeatable method for changing the behavior of thousands of people. They are able to do it again and again and again. This allows them to reinvent themselves as conditions change.

Prepare for the Long Haul

To drive successful change, we need a comprehensive strategy for driving new ways of working, and we need enough time for these new ways to become the new default behaviors. Invariably, this takes constancy of purpose, with several years of sustained effort. An absence of the long-term view leads to another common failure pattern: the lack of perseverance. We frequently see leaders who underestimate the difficulties of change and therefore think that they can change major processes in six months. Once we get into month 9 and see that there is still a long way to go, some leaders will either start to lose interest or get pulled into the latest issues of the day and lose focus. If we treat large-scale agile adoption as a check-the-box activity, it will never really take hold. Train folks? Yep, did that. Define new process? Yep, did that too. This myopic approach almost never works. If we are not fully committed over a period of several years, the new system is not likely to stick. When firms are still struggling after a year or two of trying to be agile, they often lose interest, say that "agile doesn't work here," and move on to some other big initiative. News flash—the new initiative is also not likely to work for exactly the same reasons.

Don't Forget the Personal Toll

We also have to remember the personal toll that this change will have on people and their lives. We remember an important conversation that happened at a client site that we have never forgotten because it really brought home the real day-to-day struggles that too many people have. We were speaking with an employee of a big firm that was going through the challenges of an agile transformation. As is usually the case in these situations, people were having to go above and beyond their normal duties. They have to keep everything running while also developing and operationalizing new processes and systems on top of their normal day-to-day activities. One employee told us, "I understand the need for change, and I support it. But I am a single parent, and I have three kids at home who are waiting for me. I just need to do my job, do it well, and get out of here. I can't be working long hours every day for months on this stuff."

Transformational change is going to be long, it's going to be difficult, and it is going to take a sustained effort from a wide cross section of leaders. It cannot fall on the shoulders of a few. That is just not sustainable, and it will most likely not work. We need to develop a holistic system that calls on help from across the organization to create a network effect that supports and enforces the transformation from as many angles as possible. By working together in an aligned and coordinated way through the VMO, we can successfully execute what is probably the most daunting task of any leader: driving successful organizational change.

Design and Set Up a Holistic Change Management System

Not everyone is resistant to change, some people even love it, but enough people are resistant enough to make change profoundly difficult. One chief information officer that we worked with said that he felt that "one-third of the people are with me, one-third are against me, and the other third don't care." This means that two-thirds may not be fully on board. For transformations to be successful, we need to create a system that makes it difficult for the old patterns to survive.

By *system*, we mean the broad interconnection of activities and structures that work together to accomplish a goal. We have to design and set up a delivery system so that doing things the old way is harder than doing it the new way. The waterfall system, in its entirety, is set up to define, support, enforce, and measure our traditional ways of working. Each part of the current system supports the other parts of the system. We need to do exactly the same thing for agile to succeed.

We need the entire system to support agile ways of working. Therefore, many of the current practices across a wide variety of functions will need to adapt to create the best possible environment for change to succeed. Some practices will need to change a little; some will need to change substantially. To put it another way, if we try to change as little as possible, then the chances of successful change are very low.

What does a holistic change management system look like? It would be set up so that hiring, working environments, metrics, organizational structures, process controls, contracts, performance plans, training plans, deployment processes, and lots of other functions are all set up to support, encourage, and even enforce agile behaviors and practices. Furthermore, corporate communications would help to lead the way through a strong and extended communications program. In short, we would design a system so that it would be difficult to not do agile. Here are some elements of what successful agile change management systems look like.

Start with Why—Develop a Clear Purpose and Vision for Change

Leaders will need to make a strong case for change. Why are we doing this, and why are we doing it now? What data are we seeing that supports the claims that this is needed? Leaders will need to sell the change to others in the organization, and the reasons given will need to be real. If the need is not genuine and this change is just to be like everyone else, then the chances of success will be diminished because people will not feel the importance of going above and beyond the call of duty to both run the business and also drive the change. Ultimately, individuals will support the change if they understand the need for it and also how at a personal level they will benefit. Communicating the organizational need will have to go on for quite a while, a year or two at least. The team will need to be reminded regularly of the reason for the transformation and why it is important in order to build motivation, create urgency, and drive action.

Plan and Deliver Strong Omnichannel Communications for Multiple Years

Messages about what we are doing and why we are doing it need to be communicated over and over and over again. This is another case where we cannot simply state the reason and check the box and call it done. Famed organizational change expert John Kotter says that you need to plan on communicating 10 times as much as you think should be necessary.[1] Why? People will not really hear it or pay attention to it until it impacts them directly.

In a large organization that is undergoing a transformation, it could be months or even a year before everyone is touched by the change. Every month or two, new waves of people will be impacted, and they will need to hear the message again because now it matters

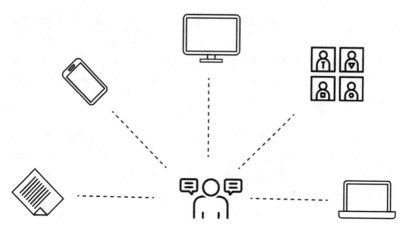

Figure 8.2: *Omnichannel communications*

to them personally. We often end up delivering the same messages over and over again but to new waves of people who are paying attention for the first time because it is just now starting to involve them directly. People are going to focus on what their leaders tell them right now, not what they said six months ago. So we need to say it again and again and again. There needs to be a constant drumbeat and constant reinforcement. Marketing and advertising people know this well. They have to create hundreds, perhaps thousands, of impressions before a would-be customer is willing to change behavior and become an actual customer. How should this communication happen? Omnichannel of course, as visualized in figure 8.2. By that, we mean that we need to use every channel available to us to get the message across. Here are some examples used by our successful clients:

- all-hands meetings
- corporate email blasts
- internal website for the initiative
- one-on-one meetings with managers
- posters hanging in the hallways
- videos playing on big-screen monitors
- guest speakers
- internal private conferences and webinars

- celebrations of success
- happy hours

Basically, we are creating a sort of internal marketing system where we are using a variety of advertising means to create impressions on the internal population. Through these many impressions, the internal population starts to become more aware of the initiative and gets more and more comfortable with the idea. From this comes interest and perhaps even desire and demand. Good advertising excites people to try something new, and this is the kind of marketing thought that we need to put into our internal communications. People are people, and the same ideas that work out in the consumer space get the internal consumer to try new ways of working.

Set Teams Up for Success with Focused Coaching

It is not enough to just say that we are going to make the change. Change will be difficult, and it will require extensive support as roles evolve. Without success at both the individual and the team levels, we will not win hearts and minds; we need to set our people and teams up to succeed. There are several ways to do this, and the primary one is through significant education. We cannot expect people to do what they do not know how to do. Training is another area where we cannot take a one-and-done approach; we have never seen that model be successful. The most successful organizations develop long-term training plans that span years. At Citizenship and Immigration Services within the U.S. Department of Homeland Security, they have developed a world-class agile education program that has been going strong for over five years. In the early days, the training was focused on agile basics. Later it evolved into DevOps, test automation, agile portfolio management, and other more advanced topics.

Training, while necessary, is not usually sufficient. To bolster the training, successful organizations also grow their coaching and consulting capability with experts who have significant real-world experience. These coaches work directly with teams to help them apply what they learned in training to the job at hand. An entire team of folks can go through the same training class and still come away with a dizzying array of different interpretations of what was said. A coach or consultant can go a long way toward translating the message into actions that are relevant to the situation.

Develop Agile-Aligned Metrics That Everyone Can Rally Around
Metrics can work to either support or undermine the transformation at multiple levels: individual, program, and organization. At the individual level, if we try to change processes but do not change the metrics by which we measure performance, then the performance metrics will usually win. If my performance plan says that I am going to be evaluated on X, Y, and Z, then that is probably what I am going to do. HR and performance management have a key role in the transformation. In addition to providing education and support as mentioned previously, we also need to provide incentives in the form of aligned performance management.

At the program level, if we continue to measure and report on traditional phase-gate performance and waterfall metrics, then we are going to get traditional phase-gate behavior. Agile is all about continuous delivery and getting feedback from users. Therefore, we need to measure the frequency of delivery and measure the collection of market feedback, or neither activity is likely to happen. Several of our clients have put in significant and nontrivial goals to help drive the change. At one Fortune 500 organization we worked with, the CIO called on the firm to "cut days per release and dollars per release in half." Another CIO that we worked with mandated that "no program will go longer than three months without delivering value to users." These kinds of agile-aligned metrics require significant changes in behavior to succeed, but they also are the following:

- relatively simple to understand
- a rallying cry that we can all get behind
- unifying in that many parts of the organization will need to participate for the outcome to be achieved

These sorts of metrics put pressure on the business to focus the functionality more narrowly and accelerate decision-making. They put pressure on agile teams to quickly develop working and tested software. They also put pressure on infrastructure, security, and deployment to find ways to accelerate the final mile of delivery.

Process metrics also need to change. Instead of measuring traditional phase gates, agile organizations need to measure things like release burndown, Sprint burndown, Sprint predictability, backlog health, and other metrics that should help drive agile behaviors.

Finally, at the organizational level, successful firms make agile adoption a measured part of the overall corporate strategy. These kinds of goals put pressure on senior leaders to drive the organizational adoption at the macro level.

CASE STUDY: A TALE OF TWO CIOS

Here are examples of how two exemplary CIOs actively drove comprehensive and effective organizational change strategies in their organizations. Both were supremely successful, and both were trying to change culture in very large organizations. Each combined a handful of techniques to simultaneously address multiple organizational barriers, as shown in table 8.1.

CIO #1: The first CIO set very high goals to "cut days per release and dollars per release in half." This is a classic audacious goal that really forces the organization to rethink their approach. It is difficult to change behavior if the same old metrics are being used to measure

Table 8.1. *A Tale of Two CIOs*

CIO #1	CIO #2
• Set big, audacious goals	• Made agile the policy
• Set up an executive action team	• Tied funding to agility
• Ensured that pilot projects were set up to win	• Ensured that pilot projects were set up to win
• Drove an omnichannel marketing campaign	• Brought in experienced consultants
• Brought in experienced consultants	• Provided extended training
• Provided extended training	• Measured process discipline

performance. A minor tweaking of the traditional process was not going to achieve the kinds of results this CIO was looking for. Note that he didn't say that the organization had to go to agile. He said that they had to cut days per release in half. He used desired outcomes to drive the change. In addition, he set up an executive action team to align on all of the changes that agile would bring to the organization. This executive team included the chief risk officer, the chief technology officer, HR, corporate real estate, and various business partners. Together, they supported one another in terms of making agile work from multiple perspectives. Then he made sure that the early pilot projects were set up to win. He made sure that the teams and product owners were committed and reliable, and he provided them with extensive training and consulting. With this level of executive support, they were able to engage corporate communications to drive a comprehensive internal marketing campaign to spread the word. He used email, hallway posters, videos, all-hands meetings, and every other channel available to overcommunicate the success. This drove the intended interest and demand for more agile. With the growth in demand, the challenge then became one of controlling and managing the use of agile so as to avoid risks and failures. However, the culture change had started to occur, and agile was now in great demand.

CIO #2: Our second CIO also used metrics to drive change within an enormous organization of immense complexity. He wanted to start the path to a more agile culture by trying to get everyone to deliver value more frequently. This CIO used the funding model to help drive the change. His approach was to not approve or fund any projects or programs that did not have a plan for delivering value to the organization at least every quarter. Since most of their programs were delivering only once or twice a year, this represented a huge acceleration in delivery. By tying funding to delivery, he was able to start to change culture almost immediately. If you want to see fast change, stop the flow of money to old ways and divert it to the new outcomes! He also changed the policy of the organization, making agile the official software development process. This move pretty much forced everyone to have to adopt an agile mindset almost immediately. To support them, he sponsored the development of a sustained agile training program and brought in many experienced consultants to help teams be successful. By and large, they were very successful due to this high level of support. He also deployed the internal PMO organization to measure and coach in the use of common agile practices. By seeing which teams were not holding frequent demonstrations of working software or not performing retrospectives and process improvement, they were able to target coaching and training to put more support where it was needed.

Both of these organizations are now world-class agile shops that are recognized leaders in agility at scale.

Position the VMO to Drive the Change

In reviewing all the preceding topics, it should be obvious that a lot of change management support is required, and it needs to be coordinated and aligned. Without strong coordination, either the actions won't happen at all or they will not be in sync with one another, leading to confusion. To effectively manage the change, we need a cross-functional group of leaders who understand agile and who are committed to making it work. They are senior enough to drive change but grounded enough to know what is happening at the team level. Sound familiar? It's the VMO.

The VMOs that we help set up and with whom we work use agile planning and delivery techniques to manage the agile change itself. These VMOs help set quarterly targets for agile adoption, help develop Sprint plans, use daily stand-ups to coordinate, and use retrospectives to help teams improve how they manage agile adoption. They use the same tools that the teams use to manage and measure their own work. In this way, they get in deep and really understand the approach, the challenges, the tools, and the process. This full immersion into agile puts them in the best position to drive the agile change for their organizations.

Summary

To find success in agile adoption, VMOs should help their organizations create a holistic system that enables behavior change. In our experience, this is the number-one predictor of success. They should engineer for success: get the right executive stakeholders on board by developing a set of change leaders and set aggressive new metrics that will force new ways of working. VMOs can help handpick projects and people and set them up to be successful. Leaders can help to ensure their success by providing them with training, consulting, and air cover. Communicate their success heavily and hold it up as an example of how to operate in the future. Look to the tools of marketing for keys on how to understand and influence the behavior of team members as consumers. To enlist them as loyal customers of agility, VMOs need to do the following:

- create many impressions
- get them to understand why your new and improved process is better than the old one
- get them comfortable with your agile process offerings
- get them to try agile, and ensure that they have a great experience when they do

Any marketing executive will tell you that it can take years to grow a new market, and so it is with agile. VMOs will need to sell it and nurture it and grow it for years, ensuring that the next wave of teams continues to be successful.

Hopefully, with this level of attention, agile will thrive and become our new way of working.

Try This: Launch a Long-Term Agile Education Program

As a first step toward designing a holistic change management system, launch a long-term agile education program. Begin by planning out the first six months' worth of orientations, formal training classes, and role-based cohort journeys. Supplement this with individual learning paths through a series of micro classes or online modules. At every three-month marker, revise the education approach on the basis of learning from the past quarter. The key goal is to get everyone learning continuously and to ensure that the learning is aligned to the desired organizational outcomes.

9 ■ Setting Up Your Agile VMO

It's time for your own VMO journey to begin! Whether you are a project or program manager, team member, executive, or other leader, you can impact the way your organization manages change and gets value to flow with agile methods.

In previous chapters, we introduced the powerful and pivotal role that the VMO plays in agile organizations and learned in depth about the elements of the VMO's work. We covered how the VMO has helped many organizations align with and accelerate their value delivery toward business outcomes.

We can assure you that investing time and effort in a VMO is a worthwhile cause. It is hard work to launch any change effort and even harder work to sustain it over the long haul, but it is well worth it when we are able to positively affect the lives of all involved through organizational success. VMO leaders who have embarked on this journey have seen indisputable results. As we saw in chapter 1, Nationwide Insurance improved business-side velocity by 67 percent, improved end-to-end cycle time by 30 percent, and reduced costs by 15 percent over a period of about 18 months.[1] A large public utility was able to accelerate their rollout of the Scaled Agile Framework (SAFe) across the organization through the VMO, achieving their initial objectives and key results (OKRs) in a year. In that organization, the VMO is now facilitating innovation and faster delivery to customers by leading the implementation of lean portfolio management. At another financial services organization, a business-led VMO successfully led an omnichannel transformation effort and achieved initial target business outcomes in about a year. They jumpstarted an agile adoption from scratch and are now working on providing a seamless customer experience across their entire customer base. Yet another organization set up a VMO in their Information Security division to help align their agile teams to mission critical risk and information security management OKRs.

In this final chapter we will discuss how you can lead your own organization in setting up a VMO to similarly manage its agile transformation and to drive customer outcomes. We will present potential VMO organizational structures for small as well as large programs. As an applied case study, we will also briefly elaborate how you can integrate the VMO with SAFe methodology.

Create the VMO as a Cross-Functional, Cross-Hierarchy Team of Teams

In a personal conversation when helping set up a VMO for his organization, a senior executive gave the VMO this goal, "When we put our foot on the pedal, we want our entire organization to move forward together." This is a simple yet powerful metaphor for the role your VMO can play. At its core, your VMO should be organized as a fulcrum that translates your organizational strategy into outcome-focused action and change.

To set your VMO up as a cross-functional, cross-silo, and cross-hierarchy leadership team of teams, you'll need to ensure that the VMO has members who function as linking pins across organizational silos and also between hierarchical levels. The VMO relies

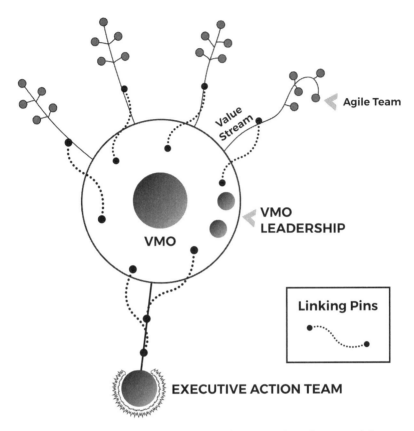

Figure 9.1: *Create the Agile VMO as a fulcrum for outcome-focused action and change*

on linking-pin members to enable multidirectional communication between and across the teams and value streams, coordinate critical work, and hold things together to move the entire organization forward. These members will have roles both in the VMO and their organizational units and will ensure tight linkages between the VMO and those organizational units. The VMO's pivotal role is conceptually illustrated in figure 9.1.

In this example, the VMO operates at a higher, value-stream level and coordinates the flow of value and ongoing organizational change efforts across multiple value streams. This particular manifestation of the VMO can work much more closely with an executive action team to conduct company-wide scenario planning and to develop organization-wide OKRs. In turn, the VMO can work with value-stream managers to develop value-stream-aligned product road maps based on those OKRs.

Ensure End-to-End Representation with Clear Roles and Responsibilities

The key roles in the VMO are director, program manager, and executive champion. Growing out from this core group, you'll need to ensure your VMO includes executive action team stakeholders, as well as value stream managers and agile team representatives from across your value streams and teams. These will likely run the gamut from product management, operations, IT, information security, architecture, sales, marketing, finance, and of course, your lines of business.

You can ensure end-to-end representation and a networked team-of-teams organization through this setup:

- **A dedicated VMO director and program manager**. The Agile VMO has its own product owner equivalent in the VMO director, and a scrum master equivalent in a program manager, who lead it in short iterations for delivery and longer cycles for long-term execution of strategy. These are usually senior managers or directors who have the authority and relationships to execute critical change work across both the business and the IT departments.
- **Linking-pin representatives**. These are of three types: executives who interface with a higher-level executive action team, value stream managers who are liaisons with the programs in their value streams, and team members who interface with agile teams. These linking pins actively serve their dual constituencies—the Agile VMO and their respective agile team, value stream, or executive action team. Typically C-level executives or their direct reports are linking pins between the executive action team and the VMO. Similarly, we often see scrum masters, product

owners, and release train engineers acting as linking pins between their teams or release trains and the VMO. Product managers generally act as linking pins between their business units and the VMO.

- **Elected team representatives**. Agile teams elect representatives to the Agile VMO. Key roles such as the scrum master, product owner, and release train engineer are elected to represent their team on the Agile VMO. This can and should be on a rolling basis, depending on whom the team considers best equipped to represent them at a particular point in the life cycle. For instance, a team might decide that a test lead is the best person to represent them as they approach a major release because she can best address product quality in VMO meetings.

These roles and typical responsibilities are detailed in table 9.1.

Establish the VMO's Meetings and Cadence

The VMO uses standard agile practices and artifacts, such as a prioritized long-term execution backlog that is created and updated in regular quarterly VMO planning meetings, a prioritized short-term backlog that is created and updated in regular VMO Sprint planning and review meetings. The VMO also needs to establish daily VMO stand-up meetings and regular tracking and monitoring events that operate on a fixed cadence.

All agile methods tap into two important fundamental concepts: timeboxing and regular cadence. Rated at the top of 100 productivity hacks,[2] timeboxing is a technique where we allocate a maximum amount of time to a planned activity. Agile teams in Scrum, extreme programming, and SAFe employ timeboxing by allocating a fixed amount of time for their work via fixed-length iterations or Sprints.

These teams also plan out a longer schedule with the timeboxes arranged in a regular rhythm, or cadence. Developing on a cadence in agile methods has deeper roots in the lean concept of "takt time."[3] Lean uses the musical concept of takt, or precise interval of time, as

Table 9.1. *Agile VMO Roles and Responsibilities*

Agile VMO Role	Sample Participant Titles	Typical Responsibilities
VMO director	Director, VP, SVP	• Set up the VMO • Assign VMO roles • Determine VMO meeting cadence, location, time
VMO program manager	Program manager, senior project manager, project manager	• Schedule VMO meetings • Run VMO meetings • Create and maintain VMO backlog
VMO executive champion	VP, SVP, CIO, COO, CEO	• Lead organizational change • Champion the VMO and agile transformation
Executive action team stakeholder	CIO, COO, CFO, CEO Business owners Project sponsors Portfolio managers	• Set strategic goals • Communicate strategic adjustments • Remove escalated impediments • Decide to start a new investment stream (e.g., epic or feature) • Decide to make a substantial pivot to an existing investment stream • Decide to stop an existing investment stream
Value stream manager	Program managers Chief product owners or agile product managers Chief scrum masters or release train engineers Agile enterprise coaches	• Manage work intake • Lead work decomposition • Prioritize work at epic or feature level on the basis of strategic goals • Measure and report on portfolio health

Table 9.1. (*continued*)

Agile VMO Role	Sample Participant Titles	Typical Responsibilities
	Enterprise architects Compliance/regulatory/risk representatives Operations Leads	• Recommend investment changes • Track financial performance and metrics • Manage resource reallocation • Highlight process improvement opportunities • Drive change management actions and communications
Agile team representative	Product owners Scrum masters or agile coaches Team representatives as needed to discuss dependencies	• Report on progress against business outcomes • Discuss potential recommended pivots • Raise impediments that cannot be resolved at the team level • Highlight dependencies on other teams or entities

a means to match production with demand. The cadence on which agile teams operate represents a heartbeat that we use to ensure that key events happen on a fixed, predictable schedule.

As you set up meetings for your VMO, you will need to employ both timeboxing for every meeting and a cadence for a core set of meetings.

Establish a VMO Stand-Up Meeting and Cadence
Just as General Stanley McChrystal's daily share-and-care meetings (see chapter 3)[4] transformed the Joint Special Operations Task Force from a siloed ineffective unit into a model for cooperation and agility, your VMO needs regular share-and-care meetings to build trust and enable cooperation across the entire value stream.

Typically, the VMO meets at least twice a week for a timeboxed VMO stand-up meeting. These can vary from 15 minutes at some organizations to 90 minutes at others, depending on the complexity and scope of the work being addressed and the time needed to address it.

This meeting begins with an information sharing portion modeled after the scrum of scrums and facilitated by the VMO program manager. Attendees review the VMO's backlog of work and quickly share news and progress about their organizational units in round-robin fashion. The VMO director and VMO sponsor regularly encourage attendees to share all news, whether it is good or bad.

After news and updates are shared by each individual in a timeboxed fashion, the VMO program manager facilitates a short, timeboxed open-ended dialogue for collective problem-solving and collaborative action across all VMO members. Action items are captured with specific actions and persons responsible, and the meeting adjourns at or before the end of the total meeting timebox.

The VMO stand-up meeting is essential at least twice weekly, and you will need to decide on what cadence you will hold it in your organization. If things are changing rapidly or the organization is in the early stages of a transformation, holding the meeting daily is quite common.

Establish Regular Retrospectives

Your VMO should engage in regular retrospectives to discover what is working, what is not working, and what actions the VMO needs to take to improve. You will also need to decide whether to hold the retrospectives quarterly or more frequently as needed. Many topics for improvement should be open to retrospection and improvement:

- team structure
- value stream design
- communications
- teamwork
- work prioritization
- goal achievement

- budget allocations
- tools

Following the retrospective, the VMO should engage in its own big room planning to align on goals and plan out its next quarter's worth of work.

Establish a Quarterly VMO Big Room Planning Meeting

As we learned in chapter 4, big room planning is a powerful way to align many teams. Your VMO will need to come together either physically or virtually in its own big room to review the past quarter's progress and results and to plan its work for the upcoming quarter.

Given that the VMO is a much smaller organization than an entire portfolio or value stream, a quarterly big room planning event for the VMO typically involves the following efforts:

- a few weeks for preparation of data on OKR key results, budgets and business scenarios by the VMO director and VMO program manager
- a few weeks for preparation of data on product delivery, and advance planning by value managers and their respective product owners and teams
- about a day with all VMO members and anyone else impacted working together in a tightly structured format
- formal presentations by the VMO executive champion and the VMO director on progress toward business outcomes and any other salient information
- formal presentations in round-robin style by each value manager on past quarter results for minimally marketable products (MMPs) and each value stream's plans and MMPs for the next quarter
- intense discussion among everyone about cross-organization impacts
- discussion of risks and dependencies and creation of mitigation steps
- development of the VMO's backlog for the next quarter

This VMO big room planning session should have the following outcome:

- clarity on the OKRs for the coming quarter
- clarity on MMPs and features to be delivered within the next quarter
- an understanding of the key dependencies and risks
- a communications plan to help manage the change
- specific action items captured in a VMO backlog, especially for executive action team stakeholders

Launch the VMO

After structuring and creating your VMO, ensuring end-to-end representation, and establishing your VMO's meetings and their cadence, you are ready to launch your VMO. Before launching the VMO with a formal kickoff meeting, an important step for the VMO is to educate leadership in agile methods and define what role they will need to play in leading the VMO and the overall transformation.

Educate Leaders First

It is likely that your leaders, including those on the executive action team and your value stream managers, will need substantial training in agile methods, scenario planning, OKR development, lean portfolio management, and the role of the VMO. A very effective way for your VMO to begin educating your leaders is to hold short three- to four-hour leadership orientation sessions to introduce them to agile and to their responsibilities. The goal for these sessions is to jump-start your leaders' understanding of the agile mindset and to give them practical tools and techniques so that they can begin to lead very quickly and effectively in the new agile structure.

Capture Organizational OKRs and Budgets

As detailed in chapter 4, the VMO needs to enable capturing strategy in actionable ways. To accomplish this, begin with scenario planning, then build out scenarios into OKRs, which will then form

Table 9.2. *Sample Agenda for a VMO Kickoff Meeting*

Agenda Item	Responsible Entity
Introduce the Agile VMO and executive action team concept and details	VMO executive champion
Briefly discuss requested commitments of all involved	VMO director
Present organizational OKRs and budgets	VMO executive action team stakeholders, VMO executive champion
Develop VMO team norms and values	VMO program manager
Review the value stream manager role, and facilitate a brief session to brainstorm the role's responsibilities	Value stream managers, VMO director and program manager
Begin to develop and prioritize backlogs and be prepared to share their near-term plans at the next VMO stand-up meeting	Value stream managers
Capture action items for the VMO, especially for the next set of meetings	VMO program manager

the basis for MMPs. You will need to facilitate one or more sessions with your executive action team to iterate on the OKRs. You will also need to get executive stakeholders to identify budget allocations at a high level for all the items in the VMO's portfolio.

Launch the VMO with a Kickoff Meeting
Launching the VMO with a kickoff meeting is an important step in setting the tone for the VMO and establishing the gravity of the work that it needs to do. Some potential elements for you to include in your agenda for this meeting are listed in table 9.2.

Launch an Agile Center of Excellence
As we saw in chapter 8, all successful transformations actively manage change. Developing a holistic system and delivering omnichannel

communication over an extended period requires focus, intention, organization, and discipline on the part of the VMO. Unlike day-to-day management of the flow of work in the portfolio, change management is a long-term and strategic leadership activity.

One of the best ways to ensure that this critical work gets implemented correctly is to create an agile center of excellence (COE) within the VMO. If you are implementing SAFe, this means setting up a lean-agile center of excellence within the VMO. Directed by and working with the appropriate executive action team stakeholder, the agile COE owns the development and execution of a holistic change management system and omnichannel communications. This ranges from agile training and coaching to scheduling, to holding regular lunch-and-learn events to showcase ongoing progress and disseminate critical information about your agile transformation. For example, the U.S. Department of Homeland Security launched an agile COE to drive agile and DevOps maturity. That COE brings in external speakers and experts once a month to ensure fresh learning and exchange of ideas.[5]

Manage the Agile Life Cycle

Once launched, your VMO will have a strategic responsibility to drive organizational change, as well as the day-to-day responsibility to help manage a dynamic, active portfolio of work. This latter aspect of the VMO's work is coordinated by the VMO program manager, who works in close concert with value stream managers to manage the active portfolio of work.

We can represent the agile life cycle for this value stream management work in two major categories, getting to ready and getting to done, as illustrated in figure 9.2. We will use a simplified version of SAFe as a working example, as detailed next.

Manage the Agile Life Cycle—Getting to Ready

Getting to ready involves significant enterprise effort across SAFe's agile release trains and teams and is a bidirectional alignment of all

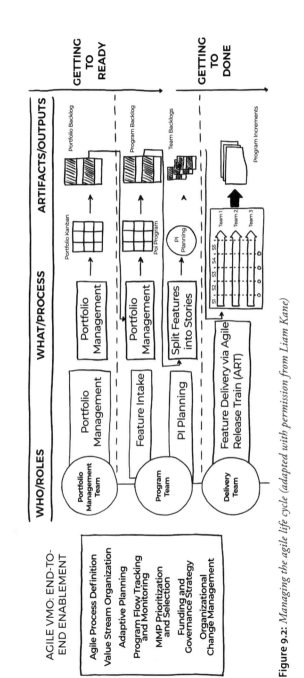

Figure 9.2: *Managing the agile life cycle (adapted with permission from Liam Kane)*

work to desired business outcomes. In the getting-to-ready set of activities, you will need to enable your leadership team to align on business goals, epics that support those business goals, and allocation of budget/resources toward the chosen epics. In support of these objectives, you will need an architectural runway that enables the development of the new capabilities and the robust delivery of new and existing capabilities. You will also need a visual management system by which to manage the flow of work itemized in table 9.3.

By executing this workflow, the VMO can gain organizational alignment on the goals, work, architecture, and allocation of capacity.

Manage the Agile Life Cycle—Getting to Done

Now that the goals of the organization have been agreed to, the next major activity is getting to done, or to put it another way, the continuous execution of the plan. The primary product delivery mechanism, or getting-to-done activity, is teams aggregated into agile release trains and aligned to customers and business outcomes via value streams. As designed in the essential SAFe construct, this keeps teams and agile release trains on a regular cadence of delivery and synchronized via a program increment.

Managing the flow of execution of work requires the major elements shown in table 9.4.

Scale Up the VMO to Multiple Levels with an Enterprise VMO

In large organizations, there may be multiple VMOs that each manage either different portfolios or part of a large portfolio. For example, in most large organizations the marketing and customer relations portfolios may be of sufficient size and complexity to each warrant its own VMO. In this example, the marketing VMO would oversee typical work related to digital marketing, corporate communications, and campaign management. In parallel, there may be another VMO for customer relations to handle all of the work related to typical functions like customer account management, billing,

Table 9.3. *The Getting-to-Ready Workflow*

Workflow Element/ Deliverable	Purpose and Details
Scenario planning and OKRs	Capture strategic themes and OKRs.
	See chapter 4 for details on how to conduct scenario planning and how to capture OKRs.
Portfolio epics and MMPs	Capture and manage most significant initiatives in a portfolio using epics and MMPs.
	See chapter 6 for details on prioritizing and selecting MMPs.
Quarterly budget	• Establish funding and governance practices to increase throughput and reduce costs.
	• Set financial guardrails around spending and other financial considerations.
	• Allocate funding to value streams.
	See chapter 7 for details on how to establish a funding and governance strategy.
Portfolio Kanban	Visualize, manage, and analyze the prioritization and flow of portfolio epics from ideation to implementation and completion:
	• Set up visual management system.
	• Track stages: funnel, reviewing, analyzing, portfolio backlog, implementing, done.
	• Measure portfolio performance in terms of flow of delivery, incremental business results.
	See chapter 5 for details on how to set up a VMS.
Architectural runway	Support continuous flow of value through automated build-and-test, continuous integration, continuous deployment and enablers.

Table 9.4. *The Getting-to-Done Workflow*

Workflow Element/ Deliverable	Purpose and Details
Program Kanban	Visualize and manage the flow of features and capabilities from ideation to analysis, implementation, and release through the continuous delivery pipeline.
Big room planning, program backlog	Help define and align value streams to strategy and develop an integrated plan.
Sprint planning, team backlogs	Further refinement at the team level for the upcoming Sprint.
Daily Scrum	Daily synchronization and impediment identification.
Scrum of Scrums and product owner sync	Synchronization and coordination across teams and across product owners.
Feature delivery on agile release trains/ teams	Track delivery of working tested software as the primary measure of progress.
Quarterly inspect and adapt	Integrate across teams and perform system demos. Perform program retrospective across teams for improvement.

and operational communications. Each VMO will have its own set of value streams that it manages using an allocated budget.

To scale up to this level with multiple value streams and multiple portfolios, we would need an enterprise VMO, as illustrated in figure 9.3. The enterprise VMO would set enterprise objectives, allocate capacity, and measure results across all functions. The enterprise VMO would also interact directly with the executive action team and serve as an integration point for the portfolio-level marketing and customer relations VMOs.

This scaling pattern and approach is common in organizations practicing agile at scale and has proved to be very successful when implemented correctly with Disciplined Agile, SAFe, and other methods.

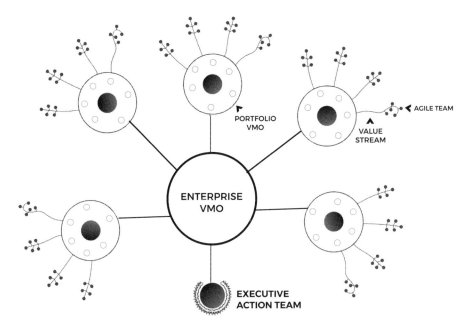

Figure 9.3: *Scaling Up the VMO to multiple levels with an enterprise VMO*

Summary

Creating your VMO as a cross-functional, cross-hierarchy team of teams, ensuring end-to-end representation with clear roles and responsibilities, establishing VMO meetings and cadence, and then launching your VMO may take several weeks and even months.

However, with the VMO set up with the right people and processes to drive change and flow work, your organization will make strides toward business agility. Reproduced from chapter 1, table 9.5 captures the VMO's responsibilities along with ways to get started now.

Once your VMO is launched, it will manage the dual elements of your larger agile life cycle, getting to ready and getting to done on a continuous basis. Should you need to scale the VMO up to handle multiple portfolios, you can design and evolve to an enterprise VMO structure as described in the preceding.

This chapter takes everything we learned in earlier chapters and provides a blueprint for you to set up a VMO in your organization.

Table 9.5. *VMO Responsibilities and Approaches*

Agile VMO Function	Responsibilities
Defining an agile process	• Establish high discipline as the driving goal for all your agile processes • Take a calibrated approach to defining your agile processes • Define metrics that support and drive dynamic transformation • Develop process controls as natural outputs of the process
Organizing around value streams	• Organize as adaptive networks of teams • Define flexible value streams by customer journeys • Establish the VMO as a team of teams • Fund experience-aligned teams by value stream
Adaptive planning	• Conform to value, rather than comply to plan • Plan, deliver, and measure in small batches • Measure business outcomes, not stage outputs • Sense and respond to business conditions • Apply adaptive planning at multiple levels • Conduct strategy planning • Conduct portfolio planning • Conduct product and release planning • Conduct Sprint/iteration and daily planning
Tracking and monitoring program flow	• Understand visual management systems • Track and monitor program flow with visual management systems • Measure and improve flow • Drive continuous learning and adaptation
Prioritizing and selecting MMPs	• Plan for a fundamental shift from project to MMP delivery • Select MMPs for maximum financial impact • Use weighted shortest job first to prioritize and select the most impactful options • Deliver the MMP and learn

Table 9.5. *(continued)*

Agile VMO Function	Responsibilities
Evolving a funding and governance strategy	• Keep your funding model flexible • Provide fixed funding for value streams • Strategize more frequently; annual is not enough • Monetize at the feature level • Devise a fixed-cost model for your stable agile teams • Adopt business outcomes as key governance controls • Utilize a lean business case • Require frequent delivery, and measure incremental business results • Recognize that it is fundamentally about the time value of money
Managing organizational change	• Recognize that change is extraordinarily difficult • Design and set up a holistic change management system • Position the VMO to drive the change

As we have stressed, the VMO is methodology agnostic, and you can implement it with Disciplined Agile or SAFe or in smaller organizations without a scaling methodology, directly with Scrum and Kanban teams.

We designed the VMO in conjunction with many of our clients to meet the specific need of ensuring that their agile transformations deliver quickly and continuously on their business outcomes. We have captured VMO in its current state, and we look forward to hearing from you so that we can continue to evolve it together. Best of luck on your VMO journey.

Preface

1. Sanjiv Augustine and Roland Cuellar, "The Lean Agile-PMO: Using Lean Thinking to Accelerate Agile Project Delivery," *Cutter Consortium* 7, no. 10 (September 30, 2006), https://www.cutter.com/article/lean-agile-pmo-using-lean-thinking-accelerate-agile-project-delivery-425491.

Chapter 1

1. Robert Klingler and Bryan Cave Leighton Paisner, "PPP Loan Statistics through June 6, 2020," JD Supra, June 9, 2020, https://www.jdsupra.com/legalnews/ppp-loan-statistics-through-june-6-2020-45420/.

2. Innosight, "2018 Corporate Longevity Forecast: Creative Destruction Is Accelerating," 2018, https://www.innosight.com/insight/creative-destruction/.

3. Melvin Conway, "Conway's Law," accessed September 15, 2020, https://www.melconway.com/Home/Conways_Law.html.

4. Behnam Tabrizi, "The Key to Change Is Middle Management," *Harvard Business Review*, November 5, 2014, https://hbr.org/2014/10/the-key-to-change-is-middle-management.

5. Mark Lines and Scott W. Ambler, *Introduction to Disciplined Agile Delivery: A Small Agile Team's Journey from Scrum to DevOps* (Newtown Square, PA: Project Management Institute, 2020).

6. Charles Kennedy and Sanjiv Augustine, "Sparking End-to-End Agility," presentation at Agile + DevOps West, Techwell, Las Vegas, NV, 2019, https://www.stickyminds.com/sites/default/files/presentation/file/2019/A17%20-%20AugustineKennedy.pdf.

Chapter 2

1. Miriam Berger and Adam Taylor, "When It Comes to Coronavirus Response, Superpowers May Need to Study Smaller Nations," *Washington Post*, May 18, 2020, https://www.washingtonpost.com/world/2020/05/16/when-it-comes-coronavirus -response-superpowers-may-need-study-smaller-nations/.

2. The Agile Alliance, "Manifesto for Agile Software Development," https:// agilemanifesto.org/.

3. Department of Homeland Security, Agile Development and Delivery for Information Technology Instruction Manual 102-02-004-01, July 15 (Washington, DC, 2016).

Chapter 3

1. "Is There a Limit to How Many Friends We Can Have?," NPR, January 13, 2017, https://www.npr.org/2017/01/13/509358157/is-there-a-limit-to-how-many-friends-we -can-have.

2. Melvin Conway, "Conway's Law," accessed September 15, 2020, https://www .melconway.com/Home/Conways_Law.html.

3. Valerie Bolden-Barrett, "Job Autonomy Directly Correlates with Employee Happiness," HR Dive, April 26, 2017, https://www.hrdive.com/news/job-autonomy -directly-correlates-with-employee-happiness/441263/.

4. Kent Beck (@KentBeck), "Autonomy without Accountability Is Just Vacation," Twitter, April 10, 2017, 8:37 a.m., https://twitter.com/kentbeck/status/851459129830850561 ?lang=en.

5. Stanley A. McChrystal, *Team of Teams: New Rules of Engagement for a Complex World* (New York: Portfolio/Penguin, 2015).

Chapter 4

1. Jeremy Hope, "Use a Rolling Forecast to Spot Trends," HBS Working Knowledge, Harvard Business School, March 13, 2006, https://hbswk.hbs.edu/archive/use -a-rolling-forecast-to-spot-trends.

2. Lars Mieritz, "Survey Shows Why Projects Fail," June 1, 2012, https://www .gartner.com/en/documents/2034616.

3. Thomas Macaulay, "How CIOs Are Using Agile Methodology," CIO, April 9, 2019, https://www.cio.com/article/3521357/how-uk-cios-are-using-agile-project -management.html.

4. Jeffrey B. Liebman and Neale Mahoney, "Do Expiring Budgets Lead to Wasteful Year-End Spending? Evidence from Federal Procurement," *American Economic Review* 107, no. 11 (2017): 3510–3549, https://doi.org/10.1257/aer.20131296.

5. Bent Flyvbjerg and Alexander Budzier, "Why Your IT Project May Be Riskier Than You Think," *Harvard Business Review*, August 1, 2014, https://hbr.org/2011/09 /why-your-it-project-may-be-riskier-than-you-think.

6. James A. Highsmith, *Agile Project Management: Creating Innovative Products* (Boston, MA: Addison-Wesley, 2004).

7. Jim Highsmith, "Beyond Scope, Schedule, and Cost: Measuring Agile Performance," *Cutter Blog*, August 10, 2009, https://blog.cutter.com/2009/08/10/beyond -scope-schedule-and-cost-measuring-agile-performance/.

8. Jeff Sutherland, "On Fighter Pilots and Product Owners," Scrum Inc., 2012, https://www.scruminc.com/on-fighter-pilots-and-product-owners/.

9. Mark Bonchek and Chris Fussell, "Decision Making, Top Gun Style," *Harvard Business Review*, August 7, 2014, https://hbr.org/2013/09/decision-making-top-gun -style.

10. Dwight D. Eisenhower, "Remarks at the National Defense Executive Reserve Conference" (speech, Washington, DC, November 14, 1957), American Presidency Project, https://www.presidency.ucsb.edu/documents/remarks-the-national-defense -executive-reserve-conference.

11. Mike Cohn, *Agile Estimating and Planning* (Upper Saddle River, NJ: Prentice Hall PTR, 2006).

12. Gabrielle Coppola, "Automakers Will Need Months to Get Factories Up and Running," Bloomberg, April 15, 2020, https://www.bloomberg.com/news/articles /2020-04-15/automakers-will-need-months-to-get-factories-back-up-and-running.

13. Giulia Pines, "The Origin Story: A Closer Look at the Man Who Invented OKRs," *What Matters*, September 9, 2020, https://www.whatmatters.com/articles /the-origin-story/.

14. Simon Sinek, "How Airbnb Pivoted | Simon Sinek & Brian Chesky" YouTube video, 3:58, August 14, 2020, https://www.youtube.com/watch?v=QddGZcBujow.

15. M. Denne and Jane Cleland-Huang, "The Incremental Funding Method: Data-Driven Software Development," *IEEE Software* 21, no. 3 (2004): 39–47, https:// doi.org/10.1109/MS.2004.1293071.

16. Ken Schwaber and Jeff Sutherland, "The Scrum Guide™," Scrum Guide | Scrum Guides, 2020, https://scrumguides.org/scrum-guide.html.

Chapter 5

1. Bob Payne, "Agile06—Bud Phillips, Vice President Capital One—Decisioning Services" Agile Toolkit Podcast, August 3, 2006, https://agiletoolkit.libsyn.com/agile06 _bud_phillips_vice_president_capital_one_decisioning_services.

2. Herman Miller, "The Motley Fool: Financial Firm Goes Its Own Way with Unconventional Space," Case Studies—Herman Miller, 2012, https://www.hermanmiller .com/research/categories/case-studies/the-motley-fool/.

3. Mik Kersten, *Project to Product: How to Survive and Thrive in the Age of Digital Disruption with the Flow Framework* (Portland, OR: IT Revolution, 2018).

Chapter 6

1. Donald G. Reinertsen, *The Principles of Product Development Flow: Second Generation Lean Product Development* (Redondo Beach, CA: Celeritas Publishing, 2009).

Chapter 7

1. Business Agility Institute, "2019 Business Agility Report: Raising the BAR," 2nd ed. (Business Agility Institute, 2019), 4.

2. "What Is the Time Value of Money?," Motley Fool, February 19, 2016, https://www.fool.com/knowledge-center/time-value-of-money.aspx.

Chapter 8

1. John Kotter, "Think You're Communicating Enough? Think Again," *Forbes Magazine*, February 10, 2012, https://www.forbes.com/sites/johnkotter/2011/06/14/think-youre-communicating-enough-think-again/.

Chapter 9

1. Charles Kennedy and Sanjiv Augustine, "Sparking End-to-End Agility," presentation at Agile + DevOps West, Techwell, Las Vegas, NV, 2019, https://www.stickyminds.com/sites/default/files/presentation/file/2019/A17%20-%20AugustineKennedy.pdf.

2. Marc Zao-Sanders, "How Timeboxing Works and Why It Will Make You More Productive," *Harvard Business Review*, January 27, 2019, https://hbr.org/2018/12/how-timeboxing-works-and-why-it-will-make-you-more-productive.

3. "Takt Time," Lean Enterprise Institute, accessed September 24, 2020, https://www.lean.org/lexicon/takt-time.

4. Ilan Mochari, "How General McChrystal's Meeting Strategy Changed a Siloed Culture," *Inc.com*, May 15, 2015, https://www.inc.com/ilan-mochari/genearl-mcchrystal-meetings.html.

5. Jason Miller, "DHS, IRS, OMB Clearing a Path to Achieve Agile Maturity," Federal News Network, May 24, 2019, https://federalnewsnetwork.com/ask-the-cio/2019/05/dhs-irs-omb-clearing-a-path-to-achieve-agile-maturity/.

6. Liam Kane, *SAFe PI Planning: A Step-By-Step Guide* (Agile One Media, 2018).

Acknowledgments

We have had the good fortune to have been in the right place at the right time when the agile movement began and to work with so many like-minded leaders over the past two decades. For those we have collaborated with, coached, consulted, mentored, and been mentored by, we thank you. We'd like to acknowledge our customers, who have put their trust in us as we work together to improve their organizations. We are grateful for the partnerships and friendships along the way.

Sincere thanks in particular to our friends from Nationwide Insurance, who have walked the agile walk with us for over a decade.

Thank you to Charlie Kennedy, our long-time client partner who has taken the time to provide us with invaluable guidance over the years and with this book. We appreciate the hours you have spent reviewing our work, the honest feedback, and the shared commitment to sharing the VMO model with the world.

To our LitheSpeed team, which has supported and inspired us beyond words as we all strive to make people's work more valued, productive, and fulfilling. We have learned so much from our colleagues.

Finally, thanks to our families. We have spent many a night locked up in our offices working or on the road traveling. Any success in our careers is the direct result of their unwavering love and support.

Index

Founder and CEO of LitheSpeed LLC and the Agile Leadership Academy, **Sanjiv Augustine** is an entrepreneur, industry-leading agile and lean expert, author, speaker, management consultant, and trainer. With 30 years in the industry, Sanjiv has served as a trusted advisor over the past 20 years to executives and management at leading firms and agencies including Capital One, the Capital Group, CNBC, Comcast,

Freddie Mac, Fannie Mae, Federal Reserve Board of Governors, General Dynamics, HCA Healthcare, the Motley Fool, National Geographic, Nationwide Insurance, PG&E, U.S. Citizenship and Immigration Services, U.S. Customs and Border Protection, U.S. Patent and Trademark Office, Walmart, and Samsung.

He is the host of the *Agile Caravanserai* podcast and author of the books *Managing Agile Projects* (Prentice-Hall 2005), *Scaling Agile: A Lean JumpStart* (2015); and several seminal publications, including "The Lean-Agile PMO: Using Lean Thinking to Accelerate Agile Project Delivery." He is the past chair of the Agile Alliance's Agile Executive Forum and the founder and moderator of the DC Lean + Agile Meetup. Sanjiv was also a founder and advisory board member of the Agile Leadership Network (ALN) and a founding member of the Project Management Institute's Agile Community of Practice.

Roland Cuellar (kway-are) is the Senior Vice President of Business Agility at LitheSpeed, where he helps large organizations move toward end-to-end agility. Roland has focused exclusively on agile software development and lean business process improvement for the last 14 years. During that time, Roland has worked with Capital One, CNBC, Westinghouse Nuclear Power, Nationwide Insurance, the Capital Group, U.S. Department of Homeland Security, the US Courts, General Dynamics, and many other clients on enterprise agile adoption. Roland has spoken at numerous conferences and has published a number of articles on the subjects of agile, portfolio management, quality, and Kanban. Roland has a BS in Computer Science from the University of Houston and an MBA from UCLA. He holds certifications as a SAFe Program Consultant (SPC) from Scaled Agile, a Certified Scrum Practitioner from Scrum Alliance, and a Lean-Six-Sigma Green Belt.

A Certified Kanban Coach and Certified Agile Leader, **Audrey Scheere** is the Senior Vice President of Training and Innovation at LitheSpeed, where she directs the team's strategic initiatives and portfolio of services. Audrey has been a project consultant for 10 years, focusing on media and communications.

Audrey has consulted on and contributed to dozens of global translation and digital content projects, from radio broadcasting to media recording and translation. As a Peace Corps Volunteer, she trained both volunteers and local counterparts in project design and management for community development and facilitated public health and IT workshops (Philippines, 2012–2014). She holds a BA in Telecommunication Media Studies from Texas A&M University and a certificate in Leading for Creativity from IDEO U.

Berrett–Koehler
BK Publishers

Berrett-Koehler is an independent publisher dedicated to an ambitious mission: *Connecting people and ideas to create a world that works for all.*

Our publications span many formats, including print, digital, audio, and video. We also offer online resources, training, and gatherings. And we will continue expanding our products and services to advance our mission.

We believe that the solutions to the world's problems will come from all of us, working at all levels: in our society, in our organizations, and in our own lives. Our publications and resources offer pathways to creating a more just, equitable, and sustainable society. They help people make their organizations more humane, democratic, diverse, and effective (and we don't think there's any contradiction there). And they guide people in creating positive change in their own lives and aligning their personal practices with their aspirations for a better world.

And we strive to practice what we preach through what we call "The BK Way." At the core of this approach is *stewardship,* a deep sense of responsibility to administer the company for the benefit of all of our stakeholder groups, including authors, customers, employees, investors, service providers, sales partners, and the communities and environment around us. Everything we do is built around stewardship and our other core values of *quality, partnership, inclusion,* and *sustainability.*

This is why Berrett-Koehler is the first book publishing company to be both a B Corporation (a rigorous certification) and a benefit corporation (a for-profit legal status), which together require us to adhere to the highest standards for corporate, social, and environmental performance. And it is why we have instituted many pioneering practices (which you can learn about at www.bkconnection.com), including the Berrett-Koehler Constitution, the Bill of Rights and Responsibilities for BK Authors, and our unique Author Days.

We are grateful to our readers, authors, and other friends who are supporting our mission. We ask you to share with us examples of how BK publications and resources are making a difference in your lives, organizations, and communities at www.bkconnection.com/impact.

Dear reader,

Thank you for picking up this book and welcome to the worldwide BK community! You're joining a special group of people who have come together to create positive change in their lives, organizations, and communities.

What's BK all about?

Our mission is to connect people and ideas to create a world that works for all.

Why? Our communities, organizations, and lives get bogged down by old paradigms of self-interest, exclusion, hierarchy, and privilege. But we believe that can change. That's why we seek the leading experts on these challenges—and share their actionable ideas with you.

A welcome gift

To help you get started, we'd like to offer you a **free copy** of one of our bestselling ebooks:

www.bkconnection.com/welcome

When you claim your **free ebook**, you'll also be subscribed to our blog.

Our freshest insights

Access the best new tools and ideas for leaders at all levels on our blog at ideas.bkconnection.com.

Sincerely,

Your friends at Berrett-Koehler

Certified

Corporation